RAISING
GIRLS

in the twenty-first century

NEW & UPDATED

Also by Steve Biddulph

Raising Boys in the 21st Century
10 Things Girls Need Most
Raising Babies: Should Under 3s Go to Nursery?
The New Manhood

With Shaaron Biddulph

The Secret of Happy Parents
The Complete Secrets of Happy Children
How Love Works

STEVE BIDDULPH

MILLION COPY WORLDWIDE BESTSELLER

RAISING GIRLS

in the twenty-first century

NEW & UPDATED

Helping our girls to grow up
wise, strong and free

Thorsons

All content in this book is for the purposes of discussion and awareness only. No advice should be taken without making your own judgement or, in the case of serious problems, seeking professional advice.

Thorsons
An imprint of HarperCollins*Publishers*
1 London Bridge Street
London SE1 9GF

www.harpercollins.co.uk

First published by HarperThorsons 2013
This edition 2019

10 9 8 7 6 5 4 3 2 1

Illustrations by Kimio Kubo. Photos courtesy of the author with the following exceptions: p 25 © Barry Durdant-Hollamby; p 26 © Anastasiia Markus/Shutterstock; p 34 © Pavels Rumme/Shutterstock; p 36 © Stocklite/Shutterstock; p 39 © Monkey Business Images/Shutterstock; p 72 © Wrangler/Shutterstock; p 90 Kim McCabe; p 96 © Harriet Atkins; p 98 © Brooke Curran; p 101 © Wolfgang Kumm/DPA/PA Images; p 108 © Gorillaimages/Shutterstock; p 110 © Monica King; p 127 © Luxorphoto/Shutterstock; p 130 © Wrangler/Shutterstock; p 132 © Alexey Lysenko/Shutterstock; p 134 © Audrey Snider-Bell/Shutterstock; p 136 © Louise Mitchell; p 144 © Claudia Veja/Shutterstock; p 148 © Ian Allenden/Alamy Stock Photo; p 156 © Asife/Shutterstock; p 162 © Gemena.com/Shutterstock; p 168 © Janet Atkins, Georgia Townley; p 180 © Oliveromg/Shutterstock; p 184 © Catalin Petolea/Shutterstock; p 189 © Shutterstock; p 205 © Pressmaster/Shutterstock; p 210 © Monkey Business Images/Shutterstock; p 216 © Michaeljung/Shutterstock; p 226 © Dotshock/Shutterstock; p 240 © Louise Mitchell; p 243 © Michaeljung/Shutterstock

Extract on pp 140–41 from Kim McCabe's *From Daughter to Woman*, Robinson 2018. Used by permission.

Section on pp 196–8 adapted with permission from the Lifeline Australia website: www.lifeline.org.au/get-help/topics/self-harm

A catalogue record of this book is available from the British Library

ISBN: 978-0-00-833978-4

Printed and bound in Great Britain by CPI Group (UK) Ltd, Croydon

MIX
Paper from
responsible sources
FSC™ C007454

This book is produced from independently certified FSC™ paper to ensure responsible forest management.

For more information visit: www.harpercollins.co.uk/green

Contents

A Flight Manual for Your Girl   1

Meet Kaycee and Genevieve   5

Part One: The Five Stages of Girlhood

1   Creating a Total Girl   15

2   Right from the Start (Birth–2 years)   27

3   Learning to Explore (2–5 years)   45

4   Getting Along with Others (5–10 years)   63

5   Finding Her Soul (10–14 years)   93

6   Preparing for Adulthood (14–18 years)   121

Part Two: Hazards and Helps: The Six Big Risk Areas and How to Navigate Them

7   The Rush We're All In   137

8   Too Sexy Too Soon   145

9   Mean Girls   171

10   Bodies, Weight and Food   183

11   Alcohol and Other Drugs   201

12   Mirror, Mirror on the Screen   209

Part Three: Girls and Their Parents

13   Girls and Their Mums   217

14   Girls and Their Dads   227

What Happened to Kaycee?   241

Special Bonus Section: Where Do I Go from Here?   245

Notes   252

Contributors and Acknowledgements   264

A Flight Manual for Your Girl

Will she fly or will she crash? It's up to you!

What's it like being a girl today? Well, as you must have noticed, it's not like when we were kids. It's different in good ways and bad. On the plus side, many girls are soaring. A huge battle has been won for the rights of girls; they can aim for a life which even their mothers couldn't have, let alone their grandmothers or the women of centuries before. Today around three out of every five girls will turn out just fine.[1] They will power along through their growing-up years, with just the odd minor challenge that we all need to help us grow, and head off into a happy adulthood. If you are reading this book, then you are the kind of parent who is motivated and open to ideas – and your daughter will likely have a great start.

But your daughter will have friends whose lives will not go at all well. One girl in five, during her teenage years, will encounter problems, usually with her mental health or – somewhat less often – with behavioural issues such as substance abuse, lawbreaking or risky sexual behaviour which will put her in jeopardy. And because the mid-teens are the peak time for hormonal activity and neurological meltdown, this age is when it will probably show up. If a girl is going to go off the rails, you will know it by fourteen.

Fortunately for this one-in-five girl, her family will mobilise. They will get help and make changes. Caring teachers, the family doctor or a counsellor might help. And that girl will 'come good'. She will pull out of the dive she is in and become stronger and more secure. Kaycee, who features early in this book and is the heroine of my *Raising Girls* talks, is a real-life instance of this. Everyone in her family made changes and her life was turned around.

So that's four out of five girls who are going to be okay. But if you're keeping count, that leaves one more. One in five, still a huge number of girls, don't do well. They have problems starting in their teens, and those problems don't go away. They will have impaired lives right into their twenties and beyond. Mental health professionals have been on full alarm mode for several years now because this is an awful lot of girls having a really terrible time. This is new, and it's a big problem. Something has gone wrong.

We've all seen this happen to girls we know. Once-rare conditions like eating disorders, or self-harm or out-of-control anxiety are now present in every classroom in the western world. Schools have teams of psychologists now. They build 'wellbeing centres' and have wellness programmes, but it's a euphemism for 'don't commit suicide'. In some schools I have visited, if a girl disappears during the day a counsellor is sent, quickly, to the railway station to check she isn't standing on the platform in a state of acute distress. These are precious kids and it's terrible to see the pain and danger they are in.

But why is this? For years I struggled to try to get across to parents what the girls I was talking to were experiencing. But here's my best attempt – it's like being out in an open wasteland, alone and exposed. There's a cold wind blowing. It's getting dark, and predators are circling. Girlhood has never felt more lonely.

Even though they have loving and devoted families, many girls today feel emotionally abandoned because their parents and teachers simply no longer have enough time or peace to really connect with them. So they are left to the wolves of the peer group, the internet, and a corporate machine that wants them insecure so they will buy more stuff. We adults have not provided what they need – in fact home and school combined have often piled on pressures and expectations that makes things worse.

From 40 years of working with families I have become convinced that a big part of the problem is the way we live. We have, little by little, slipped into an overbusy, overloaded and overwhelmed life, with some crazy values and ways of spending our time. Our daughters need something more, which we are no longer providing – rich and varied adult connection, mentoring and chances to contribute. Instead, they have taken to the online world for affirmation and comfort, but it isn't a good or caring place. Instead of finding encouragement that they belong, they are blitzed with media and have become much more pressured to achieve in every way, look good, be amazing and be perfect. The rushed way of life of today is not what humans were designed for. We feel it as adults, but our children – from the littlest toddler girl to the most sophisticated looking (but inside oh-so-fragile) teenager – are being hammered.

We have to change how we live in order to save our girls. We need more heart and time if we are to help our youngsters grow strong. It begins when they are little babies, and continues until when they are fully adult. It's made up of small things you do every day, which this book will help you to put into action.

Once you put some fences around your life and embrace happier, slower rhythms, then girlhood will be much more natural, smooth and happy. She will love and laugh through her growing-up years, and even the teens will be more adventure than angst. We will teach you all about these stages and how to make them happy and rich in the pages that follow. But the real magic is built into your girl. You just have to release it.

As we free our girls from the monster machine that life has become, we set ourselves free too. Kids change us, and for the better. So your daughter – and her friends – can learn to fly.

Good wishes and my love goes with you,
Steve Biddulph

Meet Kaycee and Genevieve

There are two girls that I would like you to meet. Their names are Kaycee and Genevieve. Both are 17, and both are in Year 12 at school. They are great kids, friendly and bright, you would enjoy talking to them.

These two have known each other since nursery. They were best friends all through primary school and everyone thought they would be that way forever. But around the time Kaycee and Genevieve moved up to secondary school, something went wrong between them. The reason is hard to say, I am not sure they could even pin it down themselves, but today, if they pass in the school corridor, there is that awkward feeling that comes from having once been friends, but no longer being so.

Kaycee and Genevieve's lives have taken very different paths. I'm going to tell you their stories, because they make really clear the dangers, and the hopes, of girlhood today.

Kaycee's Story

Let's meet Kaycee first. On first impression Kaycee seems a very grown-up 17-year-old. She wears carefully applied make-up and ultra-fashionable clothes, and she speaks fast and in a clear voice. This much confidence in a teenager may be quite genuine, but if you know young people well, you might wonder if Kaycee has possibly become 'too old too soon'. And there is something else that you might notice. It's in her manner. Her expression is world-weary. When she speaks she sounds rather cynical and hard. For a 17-year-old, *she doesn't seem to be having a lot of fun.*

Back when Kaycee was 14, something big did happen. It wasn't the stuff of newspaper headlines, but it was a significant experience that

affected the direction of her life.

Halfway through Year 9, Kaycee was invited to a classmate's birthday party. The parents hosting the party had implied a somewhat higher level of supervision than they actually provided on the night. So the party went pretty much as it would if 40 or 50 kids of varying ages were left in a house at night with lots of alcohol and no adults in sight: loud, chaotic and out of control. Kaycee found it very exciting; in particular because a boy whom she knew, Ciaran, aged 17 and two years above her in school, was there.

Kaycee and her friends had often admired Ciaran at school, with his good looks and cool demeanour, but tonight there was something different – *he was noticing her*. Then, amazingly, it got better still. He sat with her, and they talked and had a few drinks. They talked and snuggled a little in the garden. She could hardly believe her luck (it was all she could manage not to take out her phone and text someone!). After a while, Ciaran stood up, took her by the hand and led her upstairs to one of the many bedrooms in this big, fancy house apparently devoid of adults. They had sex.

It all went faster than Kaycee had imagined her first sexual experience would, and it was less tender too. Blurred by the alcohol, Kaycee's brain wasn't really working very well; she was aware though of the shift from the excited feeling of being special and the centre of Ciaran's attention, to physical discomfort and a sense of being pushed about, invaded, not really noticed as a person. When it was over, which was quite soon, Ciaran managed a kiss before straightening his clothes and leaving the room. When Kaycee got herself together and went out into the party, she felt unsure and shaky. Then she saw Ciaran, standing with a group of friends, who all looked at her and smirked. She realised in an instant that *he had been telling them of his 'conquest'*. Tears burned her face, she fled from the house and ended up in the garden, sobbing. A friend tried to comfort her, but Kaycee wouldn't say what had happened.

She went home that night in a kind of icy rage. She hated Ciaran now, and for a while boys in general. Kaycee was a spirited girl, she had been independent all her life, her busy parents valued self-sufficiency. She told no one what had happened. (When her parents finally learned about it three years later in a family counselling session, they were saddened and shocked.) But like millions of girls before her who had first sexual experiences they regretted or did not enjoy, Kaycee hid her wounds and got on with her life. But she was a changed girl.

Did the experience put her off boys? Not at all. What it put her off was *vulnerability*, being the one who was used. She began sleeping with boys on her own initiative, and on her own terms. She chose them, and she called the shots. By the age of 17, when she first spoke to a counsellor, Kaycee had had sex with seven different boys. Possibly eight, there was a night where some alcohol-affected confusion had occurred, and she wasn't sure.

Now, in Year 12, Kaycee has stabilised somewhat, she has a steady boyfriend. But she doesn't hold him in very high regard, and confides that she is 'planning to ditch him sometime soon'.

We know from research, (and from most people's recollections of their own teenage years), that Kaycee's experience is not uncommon. Perhaps, one could argue, we just need to be less uptight about teen sex and let them make their own mistakes, and learn from them. (That is also a convenient argument for those parents who prefer not to get involved, or are too busy to keep a close eye on their kids.) But let's stay with the story ...

Kaycee's life, at this point in time, isn't going very well. Her parents sought help not because of her sex life, which they were only vaguely aware of, and in a sense didn't want to know about. Their concern was that her drinking was getting out of control (she was not yet, of course, of drinking age) and she was failing at her expensive private school. She was halfway through Year 12 and the school was concerned about her poor marks and her many absences from class. The family had been advised to 'see someone' about her problems. When she arrived with her parents to meet with a counsellor, Kaycee looked angry to have been brought there. But within half an hour, and given a sympathetic listener, she was pouring out her feelings.

The family's seeking help – not just for Kaycee, but for themselves – was a brave step, and in fact proved to be a turning point. We will return to Kaycee and her parents at the very end of the book, to let you know how it all worked out.

A Marked and Sudden Change

In the last ten years there has been a big change in the lives of girls. And it's affecting them at every age, from babyhood to teens. While the same wishes and dreams are there for girls journeying towards womanhood that we had in our day, the world is forcing changes on them that are on a whole different scale. In particular, *things are beginning to happen when they are younger*.

This is a key point to keep in mind about girls' situation today, and it was first made by Maggie Hamilton in her book *What's Happening to Our Girls?* To understand our daughters, we have to realise that *their childhood is not like ours*. To put it bluntly, *our 18 is their 14. Our 14 is their ten*. That's in terms of the pressures, the behaviours, and what they are supposed to be, and act like, according to the peer norms that exist today – and our failure to protect them, for we are partly responsible. We – and that's all of us, parents, relatives, friends and society – are not supporting girlhood in the way we once did. We haven't put enough adult time and care around our daughters, or taught them well enough.

In the last ten years a greedy corporate world has realised that girls, and *especially pre-teen girls*, are a soft target. Companies saw that there were enormous profits to be made in exploiting their anxieties (or in fact creating those anxieties) about everything from skin to weight to friendship to clothes to even making it into adulthood. In boardrooms and advertising agencies, magazines and media outlets, the war on girls began. And it succeeded. Everywhere she looks, today's young girl sees messages that make her feel she is not good enough, that imprison her in cramped and narrow ideas of how she is supposed to look, think and act. Never before has girlhood been under such a sustained assault, ranging through everything from diet ads, alcohol marketing, fashion pressures, to the inroads of hard pornography into teenage bedrooms.

The result is that *many girls have lost four years of childhood peace and development.* They are being forced out of childhood when they have not yet completed it, or even fully enjoyed it. The result is girls in enormous pain and confusion. They try to act grown-up but they can't. They are filling up the mental health clinics, the police stations and emergency rooms, the alcohol and drug treatment programmes in numbers never seen before.[1]

If we are awake to what is going on, we can prevent this. Partly it's through the love we give, partly the environment we create for them with support and interests, and partly the protection from the stupid and exploitive media messages from the world around them. I have a favourite saying that has often helped me: 'We can't stop the birds of sorrow from flying through our lives, but we don't have to let them *make nests in our hair!*' We can live in this world, but we don't have to swallow everything it offers us. We can choose for ourselves and for our daughters the experiences that make us strong, happy and alive. That's what Genevieve and her parents did ...

Genevieve's Story

Genevieve, like Kaycee, is also 17, also in Year 12. On first meeting, Genevieve seems a little nervous and shy, but she soon relaxes when she gets to know you. Her conversation is full of ideas, concerns and funny stories and perspectives on things. She switches in a moment from excited child to thoughtful young adult, as is typical of someone just on the edge of womanhood. She doesn't have the tough exterior of

Kaycee, but then, perhaps she doesn't need to. Her story is a very different one.

Genevieve does not have a boyfriend right now. She would love to, but is wary; she knows that young love is not always easy. Also, she finds the boys of her own age frustratingly hard to hold a conversation with, and longs to meet more mature, communicative boys when she goes to university.

Genevieve's friends at school are a warm and friendly bunch, not the high flyers, but the quieter, more natural kids. They look out for each other and also, if there is a newcomer or someone left on the outer edges of the group, they are more likely to include them and make them welcome. As a result, they are a large, ramshackle group, slightly dorky and uncool but not too worried about it.

Genevieve did go out with a boy at 15, and this was an intense experience for her. Justin was her own age and they met early in the school year. They spent time together as often as they could, taking long walks, holding hands, having soulful conversations. He was more experienced sexually, though, and after a few months, began pressuring Genevieve to 'go further' when they were alone together. Other girls had had sex with him in the past and he really wanted this with Genevieve too.

Genevieve is close to her mother, and accustomed to talking over pretty much everything in her life with her. In fact, her mother joked that for every hour spent with Justin, Genevieve spent another hour discussing what had taken place, what he said, what it might mean, what she said back, and so on! While many girls do this detailed debriefing with their friends, Genevieve was used to discussing her innermost thoughts with her mum, and so this new problem naturally became part of their ongoing conversation. As a result, her mum was involved in dealing with this new sexual pressure on her daughter, and able to offer her help.

To her great credit, Genevieve's mum did not panic, and did not try to take control of the situation by telling Genevieve what to do. She later told me that she would, if necessary, have brought in some limits on how and where the pair could meet, since they were below the legal age, as well as the wise age, to start having sex. In other words, she would not allow her daughter, at just 15, to be out of her depth *in a situation where she might not be emotionally and physically safe*. At the same time, Genevieve's mum supported, cautiously, her wish to have a friendship with a boy. She would drive her daughter into town to meet Justin to go to a movie or meet up with friends, or bring him over to visit their house.

This remarkably sensible mother had a low-key but thoughtful response to her daughter's questions. Instead of 'laying down the law' as a first strategy, she simply helped Genevieve to explore her own wants. *What did she feel she wanted? What was her body telling her? What did she think was the course of action she would feel good about, long term?*

She did this in a quiet, casual kind of way that gave Genevieve real space to reflect. Her mum had that knack of listening intently without pressure, so that Genevieve knew that she had her full attention, and so her thoughts and feelings tumbled out effortlessly.

Genevieve's inner signals were quite clear. She really liked Justin, she liked being with him, but she felt uneasy and rather crowded when he was too physical with her. *It was all a bit too intense*. She hoped their relationship would strengthen and grow, but she wanted it to take its time. Her mother listened, and nodded, and reflected back to her daughter, 'It sounds like you really aren't ready to have sex with him, you don't want it to go that way right away?' Genevieve said no, but she was worried what would happen if she rejected Justin's advances repeatedly. They talked over how she could let Justin know her feelings and wants.

Over the next few weeks, Genevieve and Justin did have a kind of debate about this. He basically gave his own ultimatum, in response to hers, and there was a real testing of wills. Justin knew plenty of girls who, though not quite as interesting or special as Genevieve, were willing to offer him sex, and in the end, he 'walked'. Genevieve had known this was a real possibility, but that did not prevent her from feeling crushed. She was an open-hearted girl, almost totally without hardness or shell, and she took a long time to heal. But she did heal, and six months later, when Justin phoned to try to get back together, she was kind but clear in her refusal. She had moved on.

A Reality Check

When I was young I loved to travel and live in remote places. From tiny villages in Papua New Guinea to the slums of Calcutta in West Bengal. When I returned home, I was always struck by this remarkable thing: people living in tough places were happier. Life in these places was hard, but the locals still managed to laugh and be warm to each other. (When I came back to affluence, everyone seemed miserable.) *The experience convinced me: we are supposed to be happy.* We are not meant to be depressed. Especially not at 15 years of age.

Girlhood is *supposed to be fun*, with friends young and old, adventures in young love, mastery of new skills and abilities. Its dramas should be dramas of learning and growing, not being battered and damaged.

Compared to how girlhood should be, it's clear something has gone badly wrong. Millions of parents are asking, why are our daughters so stressed? What should we do, so that their lives turn out well? As you will soon see, there is plenty that we *can* do.

Part One

The Five Stages of Girlhood

Chapter 1
Creating a Total Girl

Two-year-old Mollie lifts a Tonka truck high in the air and is about to smack it down on her friend Jemima's head. Even at two, she knows this is not really in the True Spirit of Playgroup, so she glances towards where her mother is watching to see how it might go down. Her mum has seen it all and is urgently flashing her a 'don't you dare' frown. Ever ... so ... slowly, Mollie lowers the truck to the carpet and goes back to crayoning. Jemima remains blissfully unaware that anything has happened and goes on humming to herself while holding firmly onto the only yellow crayon.

Ten-year-old Elise looks at her computer screen, and sees the message bagging one of the girls in her class, a girl who is already shy and insecure. It's mean and personal, and one of her own friends just posted it. Elise chews her top lip so hard it leaves a red mark. She hates bullying, but how can she intervene and not make enemies? She heads downstairs to talk to her mum.

Fifteen-year-old Samantha pauses during the maths exam, draws a deep breath and frowns. She has almost finished, with loads of time to spare. If she keeps going, she will probably top the class; she likes maths and always does well, but then she will be seen as a 'brain', which is highly uncool, especially with boys. She knows she can just stop now and leave out the last couple of questions. Nah! she exclaims to herself, then worries if she said that out loud? Nobody seems to have noticed. She gets on and finishes the exam.

Girlhood is a lot of fun, for parents and for girls themselves, but it also has its intense times. At each stage of their growing up girls have to deal with difficult decisions. They get confused and make mistakes, but eventually they learn and grow, and out of all this they become capable and strong adult women.

For you as their parent, it helps to have a map of the country of childhood, so that you know what to expect and what to do. The map in this book is drawn from the latest findings in child development and neuroscience, family therapy and parenting education, but it also comes from talking to mothers, fathers and teachers in many countries. I never quite trust experts, unless what they say matches my own heart and passes the test of common sense. That comes from talking to lots of people. Eventually, the map becomes clearer. You feel like you know where you are.

The Five Stages of Girlhood

While each girl is unique, there is still a journey that all girls have to make to grow up well. Girls seem to be different to boys in the stages they go through, and the ages at which they happen. In the chapters to come, you can look up the age of your daughter and dive into more detail about what is happening for her. But first it's good to get the big picture and see where you are ...

Stage 1: Security – Am I safe and loved? (birth–2 years)

Human babies are the most dependent babies on Earth. Born totally defenceless, babies instinctively know that the adults around them *have* to love them, or they may not give them proper care. It's not enough just to be fed and clothed; machines could keep a baby alive, but she would not develop intelligence or kindness, she would be a very strange being indeed. It's through her parents comforting her tenderly, singing and talking to her, jiggling and tickling and loving her, that a baby girl comes fully alive, and decides that life is good. In this situation her emotional as well as her physical needs are responded to. Out of all this, she makes a fundamental decision about life: *I am loved and safe*. And she carries that inside her, always.

Stage 2: Exploring – Is the world a fun and interesting place? (2–5 years)

This stage is when a girl learns to be confident and interested in the world around her, to be smart and creative. It builds on the secure feelings from Stage 1; if people are going to stay close and care for me, I can relax and check out the toys, play in the garden, toddle out across the grass, mess about with dirt and stones and leaves.

Babies who don't feel securely attached to their mum do not explore very much, they are too afraid Mum or Dad will desert them.

This is the age when your daughter can be shown how to paint, poke, build, create and enjoy the world of things, animals and people. If the people who love her share some of these activities with her, she will pick up on their enthusiasm and pleasure in making and doing. Her brain becomes *permanently switched on to learning*. You will have taught her that life is an adventure. Strange, new and challenging things will be a joy for her for the rest of her life.

Stage 3: People skills – Can I get along with others? (5–10 years)

Other children, other adults, as well as Mum and Dad, brothers and sisters, can be difficult but are mostly fun. Your daughter finds that she can have better fun by sharing a little, giving way a little, co-operating and playing together, than if she is just on her own. This isn't possible until about three or four years of age, and even then it's hard. But by learning first from Mum or Dad, and then other people, she can work out that *she is not the* centre *of the universe*. Other people have feelings too.

Right through primary school, this most complex of skills – valuing yourself, but also valuing others and treating them with respect – is gradually being learned. Again, it builds on the earlier stages: being treated kindly, you grow kind; being treated sensitively, you grow empathy; being treated honestly, you grow honest.

She decides that mostly people are fine. I like them. Let's play! Your daughter will be a 'people person'. For the rest of her life she will know how to be with people in a happy and helpful way.

Stage 4: Finding her soul – Can I discover my deep-down self and what makes me truly happy? (10–14 years)

With the coming of puberty, a girl starts to experience a much stronger sense of being her own person, a separate and private self. She is far from being a woman, but she is no longer a child either. Like a tree in winter, she is building up reserves for when she is ready to blossom. These are the years in which she begins to strengthen the 'inside' of her deep self – who she really is. It's a time when she needs help to think about what she stands for, and cares most deeply about, and also what her interests and passions are. Often at this age a girl finds her 'spark' – something that she loves to do and which gives her joy, purpose and a creative way to make a contribution. A reason to be alive.

By gaining an identity through doing and believing, and strengthening her inner world, a girl will be freer from the need for approval that haunts many teen girls and makes them conformist and dull.

A girl's soul is like a wild animal, powerful and savvy, but wary too. It needs time and quiet to emerge. As a girl finds her soul, she will be equipped to face the big questions of life: choosing intimacy on her own terms, choosing her career path, knowing which peer group to hang around with. A girl who knows her own soul may be a gentle girl but also one who has steel in her, not easily manipulated by careless boys or false friends. She will be loyal, tough and protective of those around her. And of herself.

Stage 5: Stepping into adulthood – Can I take responsibility for my own life? (14–18 years)

At 18 your daughter begins to be a woman, and so at the age of 14 the preparation for that huge leap has to begin in earnest. It's mostly practical – here's how you manage money, driving a car, time, eating, clothes, health, safety – but it's also a powerful shift in attitude. Sometime between 14 and adulthood a girl needs some kind of marker event, a growing-up rite, an experience or even misfortune which teaches her that she is now *at the steering wheel of her own life*. That she literally holds her life in her own hands. This is a frightening realisation, but frightening in a good way. By steadying herself, and by receiving the welcome and support of older women, she can leave behind childishness or harmful gullibility, and be accountable, connected to consequences and proactive in making her life worthwhile. While life itself can deliver this realisation to a girl, leaving it to chance is a hazardous and unreliable way for it to happen. She might come to serious harm. Also, some people never grow up and their lives are self-absorbed and wasted; they drift in misery, blame everyone else and never take responsibility.

Girls have to be deliberately and proactively launched into healthy womanhood. When this is done well, the results are impressive. A girl takes charge of her life and makes her unique way in the world.

Each Stage Asks a Question

I hope you'll find the five stages clear and easy to understand. Remember that each girl is different, so the stages can vary quite a lot according to at what age they happen. Also, they overlap, because nature is efficient and starts one lesson while the other is still finishing. I hope you can live with that!

The key point is that *as your daughter completes each stage, she comes to a decision about her life*, which is going to either help or harm her. For example, imagine a girlhood where all five stages go badly. This girl would arrive at the following five decisions:

1. *Life is uncertain, and nobody loves me.*
2. *New ideas and things are frightening.*
3. *People can't be trusted, and they are impossible to get along with.*
4. *I have nothing of value inside me, I am a nobody.*
5. *Growing up is just too hard. I don't want to be an adult. I don't have any power or any choice in what happens to me. Stuff just happens.*

Those are pretty bad outcomes, but they are familiar to anyone who works with girls. Every parent can look at their daughter, and her friends, and other girls in their town and city, and see the results of these stages being lived out. Some girls will make it, some will not. The decisions that girls make at each stage are profound and life-altering.

Fortunately (in case you are now paralysed with fear!), these decisions are made little by little, combining many experiences, so we shouldn't panic about always getting things right. The stages last for years and we get lots of chances.

As a parent, *what matters is that you don't give up*. Loving your daughter and keeping on trying are what will get you through. And if your daughter is already past some of the stages and you feel that she didn't really get the message, don't despair, those decisions can often be remade later.

Of course, if you have a new little baby daughter and she is the reason you are reading this book, then you are lucky indeed. But at any age, if you have enough caring and motivation, then you can still put things right.

GIRLS DO IT DIFFERENTLY – AND FASTER

Girls develop more quickly than boys, especially in brain abilities. The oestrogen their body creates while still in the womb actually increases the rate of brain growth, and at birth they are many weeks ahead of boys.[1]

The difference increases in the first five or six years. Girls learn to speak whole sentences and control their fingers, to do neat drawings or even writing, six to twelve months sooner than boys. Girls are ready to start school about a year earlier than boys. Girls do not suffer as much separation anxiety as boys if they have to go to childcare – although this varies a lot with the individual child.

Girls enter puberty about two years sooner than boys do, turning into young women overnight when the boys seem to be standing still. And finally, they become adult sooner – girls' brain development finishes several years before boys finally get there in their early twenties! It's as if Nature says to girls: you'd better grow up ahead of the game, you will need your wits about you!

THINK OF YOUR OWN LIFE

If you are a mother, you have a huge advantage in raising a daughter – *you used to be one*. If you are a dad, it's different, but daughters don't expect their dads to be their mums, usually, so it's all right, you have a different part to play that is just as important.

If you're a mum reading this, think back to your own childhood. (It's still worth doing this if you're a dad, though the stages would have been somewhat different …)

- Did you feel safe and secure when you were a baby? Were your parents in a good place in their lives and able to really love and enjoy you?
- Were you encouraged to play, enjoy and explore the world around you? Did your parents have the time and interest to excite you and show you how good life was as a toddler?
- When you went to school, did your parents help you and show you how to get along with others? Could they get along with others themselves? Could they look out for themselves but also respect the needs of others?
- Did you find in your early teens that your unique interests were supported, or were people too busy?
- Did you find in your mid-teens that you could get to know your own soul and connection to Nature and the universe, and be strengthened in this?
- And finally, in your late teens, did you have a clear transition to being adult, where you felt that you took control of your own life, faced the consequences of your actions, and had a sense of power as well as a purpose?

Lots of questions, but you will quickly work out where you did okay and where things fell down. Perhaps that will help you know how to get it right for your daughter, and how important that is.

Using the Stages

You use the stages by asking, what age is our girl? What is the most likely big question that her life is asking, according to the stages listed above? (Always check with your own experience, rather than letting books or theories dictate your actions.) If your gut feeling is that this IS the stage she is in, you can organise the experiences and inputs to help her along. We will teach you how in the chapters to come.

Another use of the stages is 'remedial'; you can pinpoint the earlier stages that she might have missed out on, due to difficult circumstances. The nature of human beings is that we can often recover things that we missed out on, by getting them down the track. For example, adopted children from terrible backgrounds can gradually find security with their new parents. Overprotected girls who are fearful can be challenged and coaxed to show more courage. Girls with no people skills can learn to get along better, and so on. Be open to the possibility that your daughter may be a certain age in years, and a far younger age in development, if she missed out due to life circumstance during the earlier parts of her 'quest'.

CLINGY FOR A REASON

Gemma, aged ten, is very clingy and always needs cuddles and closeness from her mum.

At first, her mum finds this annoying, but then she remembers something – that she was very stressed and suffered depression when Gemma was a baby. She realises that Gemma, though really in Stage 3, is going back to complete her Stage 1 'Am I loved and safe?' She decides to really give Gemma all the hugs that she seems to need, and finds that it makes a huge difference. Her daughter relaxes more and becomes much more confident and independent within a couple of months.

UNDER STRESS, WE ALL REGRESS!

Here's a handy tip. Sometimes when a family is under stress, kids will deal with this *by dropping back a stage*. A confident five-year-old will suddenly suck her thumb and want to wrap herself up in a blanket. A 14-year-old would rather hang out with you at a party or barbecue than mix with the other kids. Or a 21-year-old will refuse to make a decision for herself and want to be told what to do.

Under stress, we all drop back a stage or two – think of those times when you just don't want to get out of bed, or just don't want to deal with people. That's quite normal from time to time. Generally, let your daughter regenerate and recuperate in this way – nobody can handle reality all of the time. You only need to worry if she doesn't seem to 'grow up' after a few days. She might need nudging out of it, or some more help to find out what is wrong.

Be sure you find out the reason why she is stressed, if there is no obvious explanation. There may be something she needs to tell you that she is finding hard to talk about.

Be gentle on yourself, too, so she can see that everyone needs nurture and to slow down. Lowering your whole family's stress levels with holidays, having one day of the week as a rest day, and less overscheduling generally, means that she won't be as likely to go into overload. Often a stressed child is an indicator that the whole family needs to slow down.

In a Nutshell

- All girls go through five stages to become a woman.
- These stages teach her the five big lessons of growing up: being secure, learning to explore, relating to other people, finding your soul, and taking charge of your life. Adult help is needed for all of these, and the adults have to know what to do.
- Parents who know the map of girlhood can organise their lives to provide what is needed.
- It's your daughter who makes the journey, but you are her coaches, caregivers and allies along the way. Taking on these roles is probably the best thing you will ever do.

Chapter 2

Right from the Start

(Birth–2 years)

It's early morning and little Lucy, just five weeks old, is lying wide awake in her cot beside her parents' bed. Her mum and dad are both asleep, in fact her dad is lightly snoring. Lucy watches the dancing shadows made by the sunlight on the wall. From time to time, she waves her arms in sheer delight. She makes happy noises, and her head turns from side to side as she takes in the wonder of the world.

After a while, Lucy starts to feel hungry. She whimpers, and her mother, ears attuned for her baby's sounds by a million years of mammalian history, wakes up, even though her husband's snoring has not disturbed her all night. *She reaches over and sleepily brings Lucy into the bed, then unbuttons a milk-swollen breast for her to suckle on. Lucy hasn't needed to get upset, so she settles happily to feed, fully alert, looking into her mum's eyes as she does so. At this age the focal length of her eyes is fixed at just the right distance to her mother's face when feeding, about 30 centimetres, anything further away is still blurred. All she needs to see clearly is that her mum is happy and content. Then she can relax too.*

Soon the day will begin. Lucy and her mum or dad will move through different activities, going down the street to the shops, perhaps meeting or dropping in on friends. There will be many changes of nappies, many feeds. But most of this time Lucy will be just lying about, or sleeping. Breastfeeding and sleeping, without any special effort, are the main events of early babyhood. And through all of this, Lucy's brain will be growing; in just this first year of life, it will double or even treble in size. It will never grow so fast or so well as in these early months, though. It is the love, smiles, songs and playful interactions and all the other myriad natural things that parents do with babies, that help it to grow.

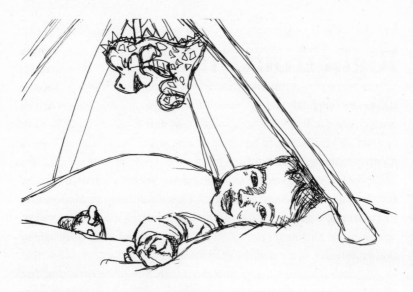

Learning to Connect

As her mum goes about her activities around the house, or at her computer, if Lucy gets lonely she will make sounds to attract her mum's attention. And her mum will answer her. While Lucy will not have words for a year or so, she and her mother know exactly what the other is communicating. Roughly translated, the conversation goes like this ...

> Baby: *'Are you there, beloved one?'*
> Mum: *'Yes, I am!'*
> Baby: *'Am I still the most important thing in your life?'*
> Mum: *'Yes, you are.'*
> Baby: *'Just checking!'*
> Mum: *'That's fine.'*

Researchers have filmed these mother-baby exchanges using special high-speed cameras, and have given them a scientific name[1]: 'Joint attention sequences' are the little rituals when mother and baby check in with each other, and they happen dozens of times a day. These mini 'conversations' help make this child not just secure in her mother's love but, as she gets older, better able to relate empathically and sensi-tively to other people. The timing is incredibly sensitive, they seem to sway and move in total harmony. Researchers found that if the mum is on a video screen, it still works, but if they introduce a mere one-second delay, *the baby completely panics.* The rhythm of *this baby* and *this mother* are totally attuned. The delicate dance of interaction, with sounds and nods, smiles and bits of sing-song, shape this little girl's abilities to relate well for life.

Often Lucy's cries will be more intense, if something has scared her or she has a moment of painful hunger, or because something is not to her liking. Her mother will match this startle response with, 'Oooh, what's wrong?' or, 'Oh dear, what's the matter?' using the higher-pitched voice that adults tend to adopt around babies. This voice is more audible to a baby's ears. (Though nobody knew that until recently audiologists learned how to measure it.) The mother will then shift her pitch and tone to a more soothing level. She will probably pick Lucy up and rock her gently to restore some rhythmic peace. From thousands of such soothings Lucy's brain will learn *the pathway from stress to relaxation*, a pathway she can use for all her life to come.

Lucy and her parents' time together will have a quality that is called 'responsiveness'. Put simply, they will be tuned in to her and will get to know her ways. They will read her signals and respond, not in a panicky way, but smoothly and contentedly. Partly this is simply how love (and the hormone of love, known as oxytocin) works, but partly it's because they have made it a priority to be not too busy or rushed in these early months. (They didn't decide to renovate the bathroom or take a big promotion right now, knowing that babyhood was a pretty demanding event on its own.) Unless Lucy's mum is numbed out by drug addic-tion, or is suffering from depression, she will most likely find Lucy delightful to be around, though certainly demanding. Parenthood may not come naturally, but it will grow and settle into a new and satisfying rhythm, if she gives it time and if she has support from those around her.

Support from grandmas, friends, aunties is very important. New mums or dads can't easily do this stage on their own, they need a bit of

mothering too. Love is like a river and it has to flow in and out of us. Being close to family and friends really helps when you have a little baby.

People Skills Start Very Young

As adults we know that people skills make a huge difference in life. We notice it most when they are not there – a hugely insensitive boss or colleague, a person in the street or a shop who is clueless and uncaring. Awareness of other people's feelings, the timing of conversation, knowing when to listen and when to speak, are complex and advanced skills. Most of us have had moments with another person where we are awkward, where perhaps the timing gets jumbled up. Hopefully this is just momentary; often it's when we are trying too hard, or wanting to impress. We lost our own 'realness'. Some people we meet are extraordinarily engaged and sensitive and we feel great to be with them, noticed and valued. For a social animal like us, harmonious interaction is central to our happiness.

That's why we start learning long before we can even speak. Interestingly, it's the *second* six months of human life that seem to matter the most. This is the time when a baby gets much more fussy about who is around them. Mothers have known for thousands of years that a newborn can be shared around, but a six-month-old baby knows exactly who its mum and dad are, and often won't trust anyone else.

Neuroscience bears this out. It's in the second six months of life that the baby grows those areas of the brain that are specifically for people skills. Girl babies have more aptitude and awareness of social connection, which is a natural strength of girls, but this still must be nurtured and strengthened. It's not a matter of being self-conscious or deliberate – that would actually get in the way – you just go with the flow. Your baby calls you, you respond. It's casual, natural, and soothing for you both.

Growing the PFC

The first six months of little Lucy's life are rather sleepy, as she just gets used to being out in the world. In the second six months things speed up. Just inside her little forehead is an area of the brain that, if you could see it, looks like a cauliflower, wrinkled and furrowed. This area, known as the prefrontal cortex, is now starting to grow. The PFC is the most complex part of the brain, and it governs some things that are very important for life. The prefrontal cortex is the seat of empathy, sociability and human contact. *It's what makes us human.*

The prefrontal cortex couldn't grow earlier, because it would have made Lucy's head too big to be safely born. And what's in there, the software, also needs to be programmed by Lucy's parents or carers, because they are unique to her family and culture and will help her live with them for the many years it will take to raise her.

Along with its social functions, the prefrontal cortex also controls two important abilities:

1. *The ability to focus, to pay attention.*
2. *The ability to calm yourself down.*

Babies can't calm themselves for one important reason: they are *wired up for panic*. In the wild (the way we used to live for a quarter of a million years) babies were carried about for most of the day, because that was the best way to keep them safe and give them good care. And often the adults were walking for much of the time, so it was just a practical necessity. (Even today, in the so-called undeveloped world, babies are rarely put down. They also rarely cry.) In our long pre-history there were plenty of predators about that would love to snatch a human baby for their dinner. So if a baby found herself alone or, worse still, a big hairy muzzle suddenly appeared in her face, dripping saliva – and it wasn't dad – she was probably in trouble. Babies who cried loudly were more likely to be rescued fast. So fearfulness and noisy panic had a survival value that became part of our design.

This alarm system in babies left alone has a very important message for us as parents. For just as we are told right from birth to keep babies *warm* – since they can't regulate their own temperature – we have to keep them *calm* because they can't regulate their emotions. So *dozens of times a day*, a baby gets upset, whimpers or cries, and her mum, dad, grandparent or sibling picks her up, soothes her, and helps her relax. 'It's okay, everything's fine, there, there.' Gradually this soothing becomes part of her, *she learns how to do it herself*, but this takes several years of receiving the gift of calmness from others. It's all gradually building into strong mental health for a lifetime.

The Gift of Calm

Your little girl learns calmness for life from the ease and comfort you bring to her early months and years. (Even in the womb, your adrenaline crosses over into her body, so a calm pregnancy can pay off in terms of giving you a more restful and happy baby.) This means planning as much as you possibly can to spend the time before and after your birth and right into the first year or two, with reduced pressure and the luxury of time with your little one.

This is so different to our idea of how to live: rush, hurry and busyness are the keystones of modern life. But our babies are Stone-Age babies, and modern madness does not serve them well. If you possibly can, make this time a break from the rush-about world you may have lived in all your life.

WHAT IS CALMNESS?

Calmness is not a character trait, it's simply a skill. You have to decide that it matters, that the quality of your presence would be better if you slowed yourself down and were really connected to people and the moment you are living in. Then you practise until gradually it becomes part of you. It benefits everyone around you – they feel peaceful and happy in your presence. It's exactly what children need in a parent. And it benefits you – with less stress hormones, you live longer and feel better. Calmness is well worth cultivating.

Calmness is made up of certain actions; breathing deeper, dropping your shoulders, settling your muscles, feeling your feet strongly planted on the ground, focusing your thoughts on the job in hand in a steady easy way, and not going off into panicked thoughts. Even just counting three or four breaths, in and out, will slow your heartbeat and calm your mind down. Calm people are actually doing these things automatically; when an emergency strikes they intentionally calm themselves *more* in order to counter the tendency to panic and do the wrong thing.

Self-regulating your level of emotional arousal is an incredibly valuable skill for life. All you have to do is notice, am I calm? If not, breathe a couple of times consciously, feel your feet on the ground, and notice how, as the last burst of adrenaline clears away, the calmness response starts to kick in. Practise this for a few days, and soon the natural appeal of calmness will pull you more and more to that peaceful and steady place. Everything is better – the taste of food, the scent of flowers, the feel of the water in your shower, warm on your skin. You will find that time slows down, and you can think more in the pause before you open your mouth. And that has *real* benefits!

Crying and Sleep

Feeling okay in the world is the first lesson you teach your baby girl. 'You are loved and precious, I am here for you, and everything is okay.' A frightened or lonely baby *won't* learn to calm herself if she is just left to cry – this is a common misunderstanding. She will go quiet eventually, but this is because of another survival pattern. 'Nobody is going to come!' A baby's prolonged cries 'in the wild' might attract danger, so if her cries are not successful after a few minutes, the baby shuts down and becomes physiologically 'depressed'. If parents are unresponsive – through suffering untreated postnatal depression, or being drunk or stoned, or just not caring – and if this happens often enough, the baby decides that 'my efforts don't have any effect on others'. This pattern will become part of how she responds to difficulty in life. It is called 'learned helplessness'.[2]

It's not a pattern you want your child to have, because she will lack a sense of mastery or hope in difficult situations. 'Depression' is often

misunderstood – it is simply an ability of the human body to shut down, from ancient times when we had to sit out bad weather or endure long winters of cold and dark. At such times, with little food about and no energy to catch it, moving little, eating little and doing little was the best way to survive. But the depression response can easily become overdeveloped. Teaching depression to a child by ignoring her is not going to help her. She may lie still, but she is actually very unhappy.

There is a middle road here; especially when getting babies to sleep, which can be an important part of parents' survival. Sometimes a baby in her cot will make sounds, trying to bring the adults to play with her after she's been put to bed. It's fine to let her whinge and whine a little as part of her giving up on 'game time' and letting sleep take over (especially when mum or dad is totally knackered and just needs a rest), but if the whingeing turns into full-voiced distress, that's not good. She needs calming and settling. The caring bond between you is endangered, and she needs to know you are there. (In the notes you will find some good reading suggestions on how to get more sleep for your baby, and for you, without using harsh methods to do so.)

You Also Have to Excite Your Baby!

After all this talk about calmness, it's important to remember the opposite message too: *we don't always want our babies calm.* Babies and toddlers also need to learn to go into higher states of excitement, to increase their emotional range and enjoyment. From time immemorial, parents and siblings will just naturally tickle, tease, excite and stimulate babies. Your little girl will giggle and 'come alive' when you energise her in whatever way works for you – singing to her, playing peek-a-boo by hiding your face behind your hand or a magazine and popping out again. Tickles, cuddles and dancing about with her in your arms will help her coordination and body sense, but don't do it for that reason, do it for the fun of it. Put some music on, and let yourself go!

Even the rough and tumble play that dads do with small children helps this along. Dads are notoriously prone to exciting kids by tossing them about, chasing and wrestling and swinging them around. Your daughter may get a little stressed by this, but if it is done in the right way (which you can tell by watching her face for signs of real distress, and backing off a little) she will get over it and start to giggle. Research has found that little girls who play with their dads when they are toddlers are much more stress-proof than those who had it all too safe and gentle![3]

(A cautionary note, especially for dads, when a baby is little, be careful with their necks – and their body generally. A baby cannot support

the weight of their head with their little neck for many months and it may flex to the point of injury or sprain. Always support their head and neck firmly as you move them about.)

There is something else even more important: setting an example of fun. Your daughter learns most by watching you. If you are happy, exuberant, silly and fun with her at those times that it is appropriate (i.e. not when driving the car), then her capacity for being happy will grow. If you are friendly to people you meet, enjoy getting your clothes on, sing while you shower, are kind to people in shops or in the street, speak well of people, get cross when you see something unjust or wrong, then your daughter will be taking in and making these attitudes her own, from a surprisingly young age.

It's worth checking up on this – especially for mums, who are the number one role model for their daughter's whole approach to life. Spend a day having a close look at yourself; *do you frown, stress, grump and hurry your way through life?* If that is so, being the mother of a newborn little girl might make you want to change that.

THE HORMONES OF LOVE

Many of us today feel unprepared for parenthood. A hundred years ago, most families had seven or eight children and their homes were noisy and crowded places, but often very happy ones. Everyone grew up with babies and toddlers around them and knew how to handle them. Today it's very different. One study found that *one-third of new parents have never held a baby* before they get their own!

Luckily our hormones help with this inexperience. New mothers' bodies flood with a hormone called prolactin. If you are lucky and can breastfeed your baby, then prolactin goes much higher in your bloodstream and makes you feel dreamy and slowed down. It helps you to focus and be there for your child. Other hormones help too; when you hug your baby, or your partner or a friend hugs you, the hormone oxytocin (the love hormone) makes you feel contented and settled.

Oxytocin is a remarkable hormone; it is released when we have an orgasm, it is released when we greet a friend, and when we eat food with someone, sitting together at a table, it increases in our bloodstream. At birth, if it's a relaxed environment and we feel safe, it floods into us. You need all the oxytocin you can get! When people talk about bonding, it's oxytocin at work. People who did not get enough love, and therefore enough oxytocin, often can be found seeking that satisfaction in other ways – through fame, doing drugs, compulsive sex, shopping, stuffing our face with unhealthy food. Or writing books!

Gabor Mate, famous for his work with drug addicts on Vancouver's East Side, says that heroin, and the rush of wellbeing as the injected drug surges into your bloodstream, is a substitute, a mimic, of being loved – but with a much different result.

It's all an attempt to get that oxytocin we didn't get in our mother's arms. So giving your baby lots of affection is a great liberator. It makes her strong and independent, and a people person who will love and be loved for the whole of her life.

HOW TO PLAY WITH A BABY

With your baby daughter, even from the very first weeks, playfulness can be at the heart of everything you do. This playful mood delights her, but it also makes ordinary tasks so much easier if she sees them as fun.

For instance, babies have to be bathed. Some parents just hurry through this briskly, but most mums and dads can't resist the urge to make it a pleasure for their baby and themselves. They make sure the room is warm; they aren't fussed about a bit of splashing; they swish the water around their baby, singing or chatting and making noises and, most, pleasurable of all, lift scoopfuls of water and pour it down her back or front, which she just loves. Many of us can still remember this from our childhood, the delight of warm soapy water on our skin, and a kindly person patting us dry with a soft towel.

At six months of age, when she can sit up, your daughter will tip water herself, squeeze a trickle from the washer, and pop soap bubbles. Bathtime can be a wonderland for her senses.

Even getting dressed, or having a nappy changed, goes better if done in a playful mood. Your daughter will fuss less because she associates this as a happy time. She will take all her cues from you; if you are stressed, she will fuss, because she is worried about you. If you are happy, she will be too.

When you play with a child you are starting something big. Child-development experts are now convinced that playing is what brings out our brain's full potential.[4] Play unleashes lifelong creativity. The greatest discoveries have been made by playful minds being inventive and different.

A girl raised with a sense of fun will not be shy or dull, she will 'think outside the box' and bring this ability to whatever career she chooses. She will be able to get along with others in a happy way, because play is all about collaboration. Playfulness makes you confident and light-hearted, willing to try new things, it dispels stress and boosts your immune system. It makes you more active, which then promotes fitness and health.

If you aren't a naturally playful person, *just have a go!* Play is as infectious as a baby's laugh. You will soon find your daughter's delight and natural capacity for fun captivates you and you both have a ball.

OUR BABY WILL FIT RIGHT IN (LOL!)

Have you ever talked with a young couple who don't have kids, but plan to?

Often couples in that first flush of confident planning, especially those who are very success driven, will proceed into parenthood full of goals and high aspirations. 'We will never ...', and 'our child will ...'. There's a lot of 'will' and 'won't' in their vocabulary, because before you have children, life actually sometimes responds to your intentions. You still have the illusion of control – something that real parents have long abandoned!

When talking to parents-to-be, it's important never to disillusion them (you should never discourage the young!). A common claim of the not-yet-but-soon-to-be-childed is that 'our baby will fit in with our lifestyle'. 'If it learns to fit in right from the start, it will be that way all along.' Experienced parents listen to these plans and do their best to contain their mirth.

I had some friends who were talking this way. They were both nurses and had put off starting a family, then when it came time to make babies, it took a while for it to happen. Finally they had their baby, and I didn't hear from them for a while.

At the time I belonged to a trauma team, helping emergency service workers after especially stressful incidents. This work sometimes happened very late at night. One night driving home through Hobart at about 2 am, I saw a strange hunchbacked figure, shambling along the waterfront near Salamanca. There was a large lump on its shoulder, and it was clutching it and walking unevenly but resolutely along the deserted street. I have an active imagination, and I immediately thought – 'It lives beneath the wharf! Creeping out at night to feast on pizza crusts, shunning the human gaze'. But as I drew closer, I recognised my friend! The hump on his shoulder was a baby. He was walking the streets with his baby at 2 am! He saw me and gave me two fingers and a grin – and I pulled over to see if he was okay. He just laughed as he read my thoughts: 'This baby is fitting in with our lifestyle!' He was walking the baby to get it to sleep, it was the only thing that worked.

Take it from me, babies do not fit in with your life. Babies *take the Kleenex of your life and roll it into a snotty ball!* If you do parenthood even half well, it will re-arrange your world. Babies do this in one especially important way (I'm not sure whether to whisper this or shout it, but here goes): *You won't come first in your own life for at least 20 years.* If you've spent 20 or 30 years being a self-centred so-and-so, you will find parenthood extremely challenging. But it will be good for you. Hopefully parenthood, and your child, will reward you with enough love that you won't mind this, but it's important to know what you are in for.

(In our family this was definitely how it was. As mentioned earlier, we planned carefully for homebirths with great midwives and doctors on standby, and both times we had emergency caesareans. But you claw back what you can – I was there both times, trying not to faint, and I held our babies the second they emerged from behind the green sheets. A few hours after my son was born, I faced down a monster nurse who wanted to put a two-foot plastic tube into his stomach for a sample 'just in case'. Our babies slept with me on the floor of the

hospital room so that they were near their mum as she recovered from her operation. So I am not saying give up your ideals, but give up your well-planned perfect life, and learn to be flexible!)

Parenthood is so worth it, and so difficult, at the same time. Say goodbye to self-absorption. You never needed it anyway. It didn't look good on you.

DON'T EDUCATE – JUST ENJOY

In recent years there has been an avalanche of products and programmes – DVDs, flashcards, books and expensive courses – to take advantage of parents' anxiety to have a smarter child. Despite all this effort and expense, with babies being urged to read at two or play the cello at four, *there is absolutely no evidence that these approaches have any benefit at all*. In fact, such educative efforts may have real costs in making parents and child more anxious and their relationship more strained. It's tempting to say that any product or place with the words 'Early Learning' in its title should be avoided at all costs. I'm not saying that, but it's tempting!

Of course babies and toddlers love stimulation, but it's how we go about it that matters. Studies of vocabulary acquisition (learning and using lots of words) have found something very interesting: kids do not get a larger vocabulary from being hammered with stimulating words and ideas. Researchers have found that the toddlers with the most words in their repertoire are the ones whose parents *listen* to them the most. It's not hearing lots of words, but using and enjoying them that fixes them in your child's memory. Children remember words when they experience the power of words to interest and engage others. 'Give me the teddy, Daddy' (Father uses the teddy to tickle his daughter, making her giggle). 'No, Daddy, give me the teddy SLOWLY.'

So we have to take the pressure out of parent-child relating. The very best thing you can do with your little girl is *enjoy her*. Chatter mindlessly to her – this really does come naturally if you let it. Singing and gooing and being funny with a baby (which is exactly what makes them prick up their ears, smile or giggle) helps her attunement to language as an exciting tool that makes people do things. An uneducated rural mother in the third world, or a teenage mother with a good sense of fun often does a better job of this than someone with a degree in business administration – *because they know how to relax and enjoy*.

What if being around babies doesn't come naturally to you? If you had a chilly or distant and uptight childhood with parents who had those attributes too? Playfulness may not come naturally at first but it will happen, if you don't worry about looking or sounding silly (because that's the point) and see what works to make your little daughter laugh and smile. She has a million years of mammalian history stored inside her, and like any kitten, puppy or wombat baby, she loves to do what develops her best – and that is play.

Not a second of babyhood is wasted. They are learning all the time and we are their teachers. These early months can feel dreamlike and unproductive to parents used to achieving all kinds of goals, but it's actually the most productive time you will ever spend.

In a Nutshell

- Little Lucy discovers that the world is a good place because her parents can be trusted.
- Babies seek reassurance from us to manage their natural anxiety. We need to organise our lives so we can be calm and emotionally present, especially in those first six months.
- The second six months of life is when your daughter acquires the basis of all her people skills – the rhythm of interaction and how to be peaceful.
- Babies also need to be excited, played with and awakened to the fun of life. Luckily that's not so hard.
- Baby-stimulation products and programmes are usually a waste of money and may even just add stress to your relationship. Don't educate, just enjoy.
- Babies don't fit into your lifestyle, you have to fit into theirs. Prepare to have your life turned on its head. Accept this and you will have a lot more fun and joy.

Chapter 3

Learning to Explore

(2–5 years)

One day your baby is on her feet, toddling, then suddenly nothing in your life is ever the same! No cat is safe, no goldfish, and no precious vase on a coffee table. (Though even crawlers could probably have got to those.)

A girl between two and five has one single purpose: to explore. This is the age when Girls Just Want to Have Fun. She does this with huge determination, and her will is strong. Being stopped annoys her greatly. Of course, sometimes she has to be stopped, but hopefully with distraction, or diversion, or sometimes with a cry of 'hands off', along with a scowly face. But in the main, exploring is what you *want* her to do, and giving her lots to explore makes for a happier and smarter girl.

Because she *is* a girl, there are extra reasons why this stage matters; in fact how you handle it is crucial. This is the time to give her the greatest range of abilities and areas of confidence that you possibly can. From nature to art to athletics, *it all gets its start between one and five.*

No Limits to Girlhood

Sometimes the limits we put on girls are totally unconscious. Just recently, a remarkable study was carried out into the way we talk to toddlers. It was discovered that without knowing it, parents talk with a different focus, and about different things, depending on the gender of their child.[1]

If he's a little boy, they say,

'Look! There are THREE rabbits in the field over there.'

If she's a girl, they say,

'Look at those CUTE rabbits!'

If it's a boy they say, 'Wow, you've made that tower TEN BLOCKS HIGH!'

If it's a girl they say, 'What a BEAUTIFUL tower you've made.'

Can you spot the difference? Boys = numbers, girls = feelings. It's totally unconscious, but it has huge implications. And what else are we changing? Nobody really knows.

Does this matter? Well, it's long been known that even though girls are equally able at maths, most boys *enjoy* maths more and go further with this subject at school, and further into those careers that need some maths (which includes a lot of the best-paid jobs). Girls are often quite frightened by maths. (And to be honest, some girls are frightened by scary male maths teachers, of whom there seemed to be a lot, at least when we were kids.)

I am sure that no parent ever sets out to disadvantage their girls around useful number skills, yet we unconsciously start making the boys practical and the girls emotionally focused.

So here's a suggestion, *perhaps we ought to reverse this.* Girls are well wired for being emotionally aware; we can encourage that, but we can also spice our chatter to them with lots of number stuff. 'How many rabbits can you see?' And our boys are already wired for spatial knowledge, so 'those rabbits are nervous, look, they've stuck their ears up to listen for us' can get them thinking about feelings. No need to get obsessive about it, I am willing to make a bet that *just reading this has already got you thinking about what you say.*

Talk to your toddler daughter about numbers, and counting, and praise her for good engineering with her Lego bricks. Don't ever assume 'girls don't ...' anything, because they can, and they will, if we believe and encourage them early on. Sally Ride, the first American woman astronaut, dedicated her life after space to getting girls to study science. It creates more opportunities for them and doubles the talent pool of good scientists, which we definitely need.

Enthusiastic Learning

Because learning and fun are the same thing for a happy child, in the years from one to five your daughter will do more self-educating than thousands of pounds in school fees could ever buy for her later on. It's very sad when parents are too busy earning in the toddler years to have time to play and do things with their littlies. And it's pretty tragic if when those kids actually get to school, the love of exploring has died inside them.

Kids learn to love life and learning from the adults around them. On top of their natural curiosity, they will also follow ours and catch our enthusiasm. Watch an experienced mother or father on a bus with a toddler and you will see that *they point things out to them with feeling*. If you are excited (or even pretend to be, just a little) she will catch your mood.

SECURITY LEADS TO EXPLORING

Though your little girl is no longer a baby, that doesn't mean she is over the 'Am I loved and safe?' stuff. In fact this still applies just as much. The reason is that *secure toddlers explore the most*. The very first experiments in child development, carried out by people like John Bowlby and the amazing explorer/researcher Mary Ainsworth, found that babies who are 'securely attached' (i.e. love and trust their mum or dad to be there) are the ones who go further and are more adventurous.[2] Toddlers who are not trusting of their parent or carer to be there for them will cling more and be less willing to go and play with a new toy or a new playmate. (Don't feel bad if your toddler is still clingy, though, as there is also a fair bit of temperament in this, some toddlers just *are* more cautious than others.)

What makes them most secure is knowing that you are always around for them.

So they can take that as a given, and spend their emotional energies on new excitements. If they are already anxious about life, new things are just too much to handle.

Think for a minute about your attitude to insects, bugs or nature in the raw. If you say 'Ick, horrible ants, aargh, get away!' then of course your daughter will be scared of them too. But if you say 'wow, have a look at this ...' she will catch your attitude. It doesn't mean she should poke into spider's nests or pick up death adders, but you can teach her a sensible interest and she will be fascinated for the rest of her life.

It's the same with machines, the insides of cars and computers, garden sheds, tools and making stuff, craft work, music making, art and sculpture, cooking, dancing, loving being in the forest or at the beach, these are all 'caught' from grown-ups around you.

Lots of Arty Stuff Is Free

The best learning aids for your one-to-five-year-old daughter are simple and cheap. Not fancy 'educational' toys or gadgets which provide all the action with batteries or flashing lights; the simpler, plainer and tougher, the better.

Arty kinds of activities are encouraged by having lots of recycled paper to hand, along with an abundant supply of pencils, crayons and paints. Cardboard boxes, egg cartons, old greeting cards and paper catalogues all lend themselves to creative playing and don't cost a penny. You can build up a considerable supply of creative materials in reserve for a rainy day or quiet time each day, and bringing out something new starts the process all over again.

But here's a hint – be sure to get these tidied away and orderly after each session, and get your daughter's help to do this. Then it's encouraging to start each new play session without having to wade through yesterday's mess. You can also alternate; crayons one day, paints the next, glue and tearing up coloured paper another, so there is more sense of new adventures to be had.

A SIMPLE ENVIRONMENT IS BEST

There is an important principle, discovered by psychologist Kim Payne, author of the wonderful book *Simplicity Parenting*,[3] which is that *a clutter of toys and materials actually makes for less play* – it's all too much choice – whereas a few simple things, in a box ready for getting out, leaves more scope for imagination. If your child's bedroom is already awash with toys, quietly take away the less favourite ones, bag or box them, for use another time. When your daughter looks at a sea of teddies, dolls, games and bits of creation cascading all over the floor or all over her room, she feels the way you do – exhausted. And really, does anyone need more than two teddies? Well, okay, three.

Clothes

Girls should have plenty of old and tough clothes so they can be messy and happy in the dirt, or doing art activities with paint, water and glue and not freaking out about getting it on themselves or their clothes. In fact, little girls don't need fragile or fancy clothes at all. Those fashionable frilly numbers really have no purpose for little girls except to make them anxious about how they look. Fashion on children is for the adults' benefit, and if your child doesn't look cute enough already in a t-shirt and rompers, then you need to read fewer magazines. (There is nothing sadder than seeing a toddler dressed in such prissy and 'feminine' clothing that she can't do anything but sit and be 'good'.)

One mum told me recently: 'I used to say to my toddler daughter, "That dress looks gorgeous" or "How pretty you look." But I have started to say: "Let's put on these strong trainers (or wellies) so you can run and play."'

MATILDA LEARNS NOT TO BE FEARFUL

(This story was told to me by my psychotherapy teacher, Bob Goulding, at the Western Institute in the 1980s. Bob was the grandfather in the story. He was a wonderful man.)

Two-year-old Matilda was enjoying playing around the swimming pool, carefully watched by her mum and grandparents. She would play happily in the toddler pool, but from time to time she would wander across to the deeper pool for a closer look. Suddenly, she simply stepped from the edge and completely disappeared into the deep water. Her grandfather, fortunately wearing some old shorts, jumped straight after her. He grabbed Matilda immediately and pulled her out. Matilda, still utterly surprised, screwed up her face and was clearly about to start wailing. But before that could happen, her granddad did an interesting thing. Holding her at arm's length, he shouted 'Wow! Matilda swims! What a great swimmer she is! You are great!' while laughing and looking very pleased. Matilda seemed to hesitate, look at him for a puzzled moment – he was hard to ignore – then she did a remarkable thing. She simply changed her face to a big smile, and joined in the laughter.

Her mum came and took over, carrying Matilda back into the water and played with her, anchoring the experience into a positive one.

Would this turn Matilda into a risk taker? We don't think so, it was scary enough to have taken that sudden plunge, but it would have taught her that adventures can be taken on the chin, and it's better to laugh than cry. In her brain the pathways towards quick recovery and resilience were beginning to be put in place.

If we didn't have pool fences, it might make sense to terrify kids about water. (Aboriginal parenting traditionally involved terrifying children about monsters that lurked beyond the firelight at nighttime, because it *was* important they didn't stray. In my Yorkshire childhood we were half-laughingly warned about the Bogey Man.) Helping our daughters to see life as an adventure and to be confident in their own skills and judgement is important because it means they can *live a larger life*. These will be the girls who scuba dive, volunteer for Médecins Sans Frontières, learn to pilot a plane, or play gypsy violin in an indie rock band. Although, I am trying to talk you *into* this!

If Matilda's mum or dad had freaked out, started yelling and carrying on, after Matilda's unexpected dip, this little girl would have added to her own already considerable startle that the parental message was that water is scary. She may well have become phobic of water and swimming itself as a result. 'Hell's bells', she thinks, 'even Mum and Dad are terrified!'

The direct teaching that her grandfather offered – 'look here, this is fun!' – can be applied to many things in life, and from a very early age. We can help our daughters to be comfortable with animals, nature, climbing, books and libraries, sporting exertions, people, the night sky, the ocean, the list goes on. And they will carry this love of the world into their lives forever. Whenever you show her a new experience, you can add some enthusiasm, some 'Hey look – isn't this great?', so that she also takes in a positive message.

Be sensible about it, but see if you can extend your daughter's boundaries every chance you get.

Nature Is Essential

A garden with real plants and soil, water, and maybe some trees is great. A rough cubby house (or even a big cardboard box) creates a base to play from and in. Gardens naturally come equipped with insects, lizards and birds, though you can perhaps still add an old safe dog.

Girls need a chance to move around in nature. If you live in a block of flats or have no garden, get to the park, countryside or coast whenever you get the chance. Let them experience the rough textures and long-distance views, as toddler eyes need to look long distances and absorb natural sunlight to develop good vision. Running about on uneven surfaces will also make their legs flexible and strong. The sheer mystery of what's behind that bush or tall grass will help their imaginations too.

Computers, iPads and DVDs have their place, but for small children through to teens these electronic devices can warp the senses and affect brain development negatively, because they are all flat and clean and the same distance away. You don't refocus your eyes or move about enough to develop the balance and activity centres of the brain. And you don't really feel love and connection to an animal on a screen in the same way as something you can touch and hug.

Three Should Be Free

With girls of age three or four, the goal and need of her brain is to play, to not be pressured and to be able to be creative and free. These qualities will one day make her a great scientist, boss, artist, problem-solver or friend. She will always want to and be able to 'do her own thing'. But if she is made to perform – by a pre-school with 'early learning goals', or a parent who wants her to play violin, or some activity that grooms and preens her for adult consumption (participating in child beauty contests is a stunningly awful example), then she will not develop properly, will be cramped and tense and lack creativity. Whole nations have experienced this through over-demanding schooling for the under-sixes. The result is a total lack of creativity, a population that is cowed, conformist and compliant. By six or seven, a girl is ready for some (not too much) serious learning imposed from the outside. Her brain has moved on to a whole different stage. If it comes too soon, though, it actually harms her intellect, and her eventual ability to be talented and bright.

So think twice about structured or organised activities that involve any kind of performance or competition. These just take the joy out of something she would otherwise have loved. Activities where all the kids simply get into it together and learn happily at their own pace are much preferred.

A final note – the two to five years are exhausting, and you can be a bit isolated. Don't think you have to be an education ringmaster for your kids all day. They need to occupy themselves, dream and dawdle as their imagination grows. It's in the gaps and quiet times that children do their growing. Turn off TVs and radios so they can think and talk internally, which they love and need to do as they play.

Don't let yourself get lonely, either. Join a playgroup, where the kids start to have fun with others, and YOU get to be with other mums or dads (there are dads' playgroups too now). Also learn to be boring sometimes and encourage your kids to just play around and without you while you merge into the furniture. You need your rest.

Choosing Toys

If you have heard ANYTHING about getting girls off to a good start, it's probably been about 'gender-stereotyped toys'. The role of toys in widening, or limiting, your little girl's play choices is a huge thing, and you'd think by now companies would have really got past this. But here's the bad news: *it's getting worse.* Companies never give up on trying to hook kids and parents with heavy marketing – especially on TV, where toys can be made to look so much better than they really are.

This article is by Paula Joye, a journalist and fashion columnist, website publisher and a very sensible mum. I couldn't put it better ...

Role Model or Pole Model?, by Paula Joye

My youngest daughter is five and spent the weekend penning a Christmas Wish List to Santa. Nestled between a backpack shaped like a koala and a detective magnifying glass is a request for a Bratz Masquerade toy. She saw it advertised while watching *Finding Nemo* on television. The doll is dressed in an outfit that would look great wrapped around a pole. She has swishy, knee-length hair with pastel streaks, hoop earrings and more black kohl eyeliner than a Kardashian.

I'm a little stuck because we don't have any Bratz in our house. I'm not sure exactly what I don't like about them. I loathe the lollipop heads and cushion pouts. Hate the heavy make-up. But I think what upsets me the most is their wardrobes. Seriously, these dolls wrote the rules on Red Light. A toy designed for five- to 10-year-old girls shouldn't be so overtly sexy. Pretty, geeky, smart, ugly are all fine but scantily clad dolls should be reserved for lonely grown men who can't get real girlfriends.

For me the message is just too narrow. The Bratz brand is 13 years old, which means the original crash-test consumers are just starting to flex their fashion chops. On the weekend, I watched some of these girls heading into the Eminem concert in Sydney. They were wearing clothes that defy description. Mainly because there was so little fabric covering their bodies that I'm struggling to come up with words other than naked and nude to describe how they looked. This is the first batch of young women to have been influenced by a society hell bent on fast-tracking them into womanhood and the first place we're going to see the results is in the fashion choices they make. What struck me more than the bare skin was how homogenised their look was. Everyone was dressed identically. It was a sea of tiny, cut-off denim shorts and fluro crop tops. Teenagers have always copied one another – it's normal to dress the same way as your friends – but there used to be so much more diversity and self-expression. I remember copying the wardrobes of Madonna, Wendy James and Diane Keaton at the same age. I experimented all the time. But there was none of that in this crowd. It was Same. Same. Sexy. Same.

We can't blame this on Bratz or Barbie alone – there are so many influences that play on young girls – but it does make you despondent about the serious lack of role models both on the toy shelf and in the mainstream. Once they wave bye-bye to Dora and Angelina the choices are whittled down to Bindi Irwin, Harry Potter's Hermione and a couple of exceptions on Nickelodeon. Otherwise it's Miley, Taylor, Selena and The Biebs. Where are Pippi Longstocking and Nancy Drew? Why isn't there a Kate Winslet for Tweens?

It would be so easy for me to capitulate on the Bratz present. Seeing her little face light up when she opens it on Christmas morning is a tempting trade. But every time I teeter, I close my eyes and visualise her dressing the doll up in its miniature thigh-high boots, a micro-mini skirt and green boob tube and ... well, I want more.

More imagination from the toy manufacturer, more depth from the doll and frankly a little bit more fabric for my money.

Paula Joye is editor of www.lifestyled.com.au.

There is something really important to say here about dolls. In Steiner Education, where kids are rarely rushed and a lot of thought goes into stages and ages, they have dolls with no faces. These toys are just blank and plain, with perhaps some simple clothes. The amazing thing is – kids love them. What happens is that the child at play puts all her own imagination into the feelings the doll might have, what it might look like, and what it does.

The doll doesn't programme the child. These dolls are the ones taken to bed at night with them, tucked in, and used to play out all their dreams, imaginings and fears. It's the very opposite of a Bratz doll. For little children, boys and girls, the less corporate their toys, and the more natural and brand-less, the better.

Finally, no toy advice would be complete without a word about Lego. There is no doubt about it, Mr Lego, if there was one, was a genius. He deserves a Nobel Prize. There is no construction toy that comes close in its almost planetary popularity, usefulness and general magic. It can stimulate minds in different versions from babies to tech-headed teens – and it benefits and is loved by girls just as much as boys, given the chance.

But recently Lego got kidnapped by the marketers, who decided a girls' version was needed. Listen to what they came up with: five curvy little friends who bake, home-make, decorate, hairstyle and shop! Anything gender limiting in that little selection?

Boys' Lego, on the other hand, is about firefighting, space exploration, knights in armour, buildings, cars, houses and furniture and ANYTHING YOU WANT TO MAKE IT. Boys play in Lego World, whereas girls play in their own little ghetto called Heartlake City! (No firefighters or policemen there, they have to get the boys over if the beauty salon catches fire!) Naturally when this new product line came out, women rose up in outrage. One angry writer summed up this in one neat sentence. There IS a girls' version – it's called … Lego.

There's no doubt Lego did their research, spending millions and taking years. Their head researcher told a Danish newspaper that they found that girls had a single overwhelming preoccupation – with BEAUTY. That's what the new girls' Lego was built around. Girls wanted to project themselves into dolls who were being, or getting made, beautiful. Now I am not arguing with their finding, but that's a measure of how DAMAGED girls are now. 'How do I look?' is their strongest interest. If you want this to be your daughter's preoccupation, then girls' Lego is for you.

So by all means get your daughter Lego, but not the girls' version. Not the pink and purple beauty salon or the café. Sure, she might build those of her own choice, but she might prefer rockets, castles, cannons, horses, trees, trucks and farms. And that would be a real shame not to have the scope for.

MAKING HER STRONG

Raising a Strong Girl Starts Young

If you are lucky, you will know some strong women. They stand up for themselves and other people. They don't quit under stress. They are someone you'd want on your side if the going got tough. How did those women get to be strong? Were they born that way? Usually the answer is no; they became strong because they *had to*.

Some girls growing up have to face enormous adversity and hardship, such as the illness of a parent, a death or an accident, or having to leave one's home country because of war or persecution. These women, with a combination of outer support and inner resources, often discover a strength inside themselves.

Most of us take smaller steps through life and gradually grow strong. We go to a new school where we don't know anyone, we face needles and blood tests at the doctors, we stand in front of a classroom or an interview panel, we keep our commitments even when we are tired or sick. Gradually life teaches us that we can get through things.

But there is a third way; one which is safer and probably the best. *We can be raised to be strong*. We can help our girls get there, and a big part of parenthood is doing this. Not by mistreating them or making them hard, but by helping them kindly to handle tougher and tougher things.

Seeing Things Through

It begins with learning to help and be a part of the family team. How you do it has to be appropriate and right for the age of your child.

- With toddler Matilda, her mum always has a bedtime routine. She has a wash, does her teeth, then tidies up her things before a story in bed.

- With pre-schooler Amy, her mum expects her to help clean up after dinner by bringing the plates to the dishwasher, then tidy away her toys and put her dirty clothes in the laundry basket.
- School-age Mandy looks after the dog, gets its food and water, brings it in at nighttime, and walks it with her dad a couple of times a week.
- Teenage Erin goes to her job at the library three nights after school to earn money for the school trip.
- University student Myriam cooks the family's meal on the three nights a week when her mother and father both work late.

While it takes a bit of time to get kids doing things for themselves, it really pays off by the time they are at school or become teenagers. By then they will naturally feel capable and know they are indispensable to their families.

Getting Your Daughter to Co-operate

When we tell a toddler to do something, sometimes they obey, often they don't. Start with a simple request, and engage with her as you make it, looking her in the eye. If she doesn't get started, give her a sterner warning. Sometimes that works. When it doesn't, we have to follow through.

Some people yell or threaten, or else give up and let it drop. Neither teaches a child very much.

Imagine your child has done something 'naughty' – disobeyed, hit somebody, broken something in a tantrum, drawn all over the bathroom with felt pens – in that situation we would take them to a place that's away from distractions – a corner, a wall, a nook somewhere – and tell them to stand there and talk to us. If they don't co-operate, we tell them to stay there until they can. (With a really stroppy toddler, you might have to carry them there, or hold them there.) Wait until they say they are ready to deal with you.

Zara is three …

Parent: Are you ready to talk?

Zara: Yes. (Mumble, grumble …)

Parent: Tell me what you think you did that was a problem?

Zara: Nothing.

Parent: Do you need more time to think about it?

Zara: I hit Elly.

Parent: Yes. That's right. You shouldn't hit people.

Zara: (Mumble, grumble …)

Parent: What are you saying?

Zara: She had my dolly.

Parent: Well, we can talk to her in a while. But this is about not hitting. What are you going to do to fix it?

Zara: I want a drink of water.

Parent: Right now we are fixing what you did wrong.

Zara: I'm sorry.

Parent: So are you wanting to go and say sorry to Elly?

Zara: Yes.

Parent: And what will you do different next time?

Zara: Not hit Elly.

Parent: Great! You figured that out really well.

Some people think discipline is about 'winning' or 'beating' your child. But that's not the goal – you actually want to make them stronger. To help them be clearer about how to handle themselves, their emotions, and be able to think really well even when they have strong feelings. (In our book *The Secret of Happy Children*[4] you can read more about this 'stand and think' method – it applies equally to girls and boys.)

TEACHING HER TO GET IT RIGHT

There is a lot of helping and teaching in discipline – it's not about conflict. When something isn't working, or an opportunity comes up, you simply move into showing her how to go about things …

Let's say Lily has started screaming loudly at her brother to give her a turn on the slide.

Lily is two, her brother is six. Her mum takes her away for a second to calm down.

Then she says: 'Come with me, let's have another go.'

They go over to her big brother who is still on the slide.

She crouches down and asks Lily to say, 'Please can I go on the slide, Jake?'

She says it for her, so Lily knows what to do.

Then, she coaches her to do it herself, politely but clearly.

The next time, when she comes to complain, we check with her: 'Did you speak up loudly and clearly and politely to your brother?'

Of course you will also be talking to her brother about sharing and encouraging his little sister to play. He might be a few years older, and for him the lesson is how to get along and have more fun by co-operating. Lily's lesson, though, is just 'ask, don't scream!'

There's always a sequence in teaching a child:

Do it for them.
Do it with them.
Watch while they do it.
Let them do it themselves.

IT'S ALL ABOUT UNDERSTANDING NEEDS

Everyone has needs. Lily needs to notice that screaming doesn't work and it just makes everyone annoyed with her. She needs to learn to use words clearly and well. For a toddler, that's a big step. Her brother (at six) needs to be able to listen, explain, share and understand that toddlers have less patience. And you as her parent need to be able to preserve your hearing and peace of mind – toddlers shriek very loudly unless taught not to.

With little children, this teaching is done 'live' and on the spot; by the time the teens come along, it is done in discussion away from the situation. It's more about rules, and consequences. Teenagers might need to make it up to the person they hurt, or suffer the loss of some privilege, or rebuild trust by proving they can stick to what they have promised.

A POSITIVE MOOD

Often in our own childhoods, people did discipline with a lot of yelling or blaming. It was angry and unpleasant. Real discipline isn't like that. You need to do it with patience and encouragement. You have a dual aim all through this: that they will become independent, which is what you want and they want too; and that one day you will be great friends because you helped to get them there in good heart.

WHEN IT COUNTS

The aim of discipline isn't to have compliant kids. The aim is that when you are not there, or long gone, they will have inner backbone and be able to be strong and self-believing. One day, it's almost certain, your daughter is going to be somewhere late at night where people have been drinking. Someone is going to want them to go somewhere else in a car. They will be drunk or stoned beyond belief, everyone will be laughing, and her friends will be saying, 'Come on, let's go.'

She will reach inside herself and find some backbone. She'll say, 'I don't want to go with him, he's drunk'. Or, 'Come on guys, I want to stay alive, let's go back inside and call a cab.'

In our work we've talked to kids who are paraplegic or brain injured or had friends die in a car, or were raped after going with strangers to somewhere far from help. Inevitably they say, 'I didn't think anything bad would happen' or, essentially, 'I was confused and didn't take charge of myself'. Discipline teaches you to think well under pressure, and to speak up for yourself. It teaches you how to have boundaries. In short, how to be strong.

If you can say to your child 'I'm not comfortable about that', 'That's wrong', then they will be able to use those very same words one day in a situation where they really need to. It's a very great gift that every young person needs.

In a Nutshell

- The years from one to three are for exploring. Give your daughter lots to explore, make and do. Add your enthusiasm and energy to show her it's okay to be messy, into everything and playful.
- A garden really helps, and being in nature is vital.
- Dress her in clothes that are tough and damage proof, so she is free to be herself.
- Have lots of cardboard, paper, paints and crayons around the house.
- She might be destined to be an athlete, scientist, artist or engineer – encourage whatever she shows an interest in.
- Don't have too many toys, and simplify her play space to make it more inviting.
- She might be nurturing by nature, or not. Simple blank dolls or teddy bears are enough to stimulate this side of her, and she can make up her own games.
- Avoid toys that tell your daughter it's all about looks and clothes. In fact, avoid anything aimed just at girls. The world does that quite enough already.
- Doing discipline with girls, kindly but firmly, ensures they will grow a backbone and be able to be competent and strong when it counts.

Chapter 4

Getting Along with Others

(5–10 years)

Making Friends

Friends are important to most of us, but for girls, *they are like the oxygen they breathe*. At age five or six, when most girls go to school, friends are who they rely on for company, comfort and fun. Parents of daughters sigh with relief when they find a friend or two that they can really count on.

Of course, friends can also be a source of pain. Nine times out of ten, if your daughter comes to you in tears it will be because of something going on in her social world. (Boys seem so much more relaxed about it all. A small boy can fight with a friend – and I mean, really *fight* – but be best mates again an hour later. Some girls can still be worried on Friday that someone frowned on Monday and they don't know the reason why!)

The fact is, human relationships are so complex that it takes decades to learn how to get them right. You and I are still learning. So your daughter will need your help. As her main anchor back at home, you will find yourself helping her to figure out 'what went wrong?', salving wounds, reassuring her, and sending her back out there to try again. Getting along with people is one of the most important things we help

our kids to learn. Nothing has more effect on her future happiness and success at life. In this chapter, we'll help you understand the skills of friendship, so you can teach her.

How Friendship Grows

Babies are fascinated by other babies, but they don't really play together – mum and dad are just so much better fun. In toddlerhood, though, a child in a playgroup will often fix on another child with great intensity and will shower affection on their chosen target (who may have no say in the matter!). Under-threes can't actually co-operate with each other for more than a few minutes (at least, without a referee!) but they have at least noticed each other. The journey to friendship has begun.

By age four or five, most girls can play together well. What they most enjoy is imaginative play – games of make-believe. It's astonishing how much of a magical world they can dream up, with very little in the way of props. New Zealand's much-loved performers the Topp Twins were interviewed recently about their childhood on a 1950s dairy farm.[1] They didn't have a lot of toys – but each had a sturdy stick, polished from long use, with a piece of rope tied to one end which served as the reins – because these sticks were their horses! Their dad would send the pair up to the back paddock to check a water trough, gravely advising them to 'ride' to save time. And they always tied their steeds to the railing when they got home.

Make-believe isn't just about passing the time; it is the basis of all creativity – without it there would be no books, movies, music or science. Nothing happens that isn't imagined first. Your daughter's playing happily by herself, or with friends, is the greatest brain development activity she will ever have.

Playing *together* involves a whole new set of skills. A girl playing on her own can call the shots because her teddies are not going to argue back. But to play together, children must negotiate a *shared* fantasy world – you can't be the queen of the pirates without a crew. If you are too much of a control freak, they will mutiny and sail away. Sneak a listen to girls at play and half of the time it's negotiation over who gets the plum roles!

Play is where we learn to relate to one another. In his book *The Wonder of Girls*,[2] Michael Gurian tells a story about taking his daughters to the park. They are seven and four, and have brought their soft-toy animals along with them. It's early and there is no one else around, the girls commandeer the big wooden pirate ship in the centre of the playground and settle into an engaging game.

Suddenly a mum arrives with two boys. The boys are about the same age – he guesses five and eight. The boys noisily rush onto the boat. Their loudness and shouting disrupts the quiet play of the girls and their animals, and the girls stand off to one side, unsure what to do. They make a few attempts to restart their game, but the boys' domination of the space makes it hard to do.

Gurian is a boy expert, and he tries his best to be understanding, but he is quite angry. It's a real feminist moment (you'll notice my use of the word 'domination' in the paragraph above). A high horse begs to be mounted here, but as he watches, unsure what to do, something interesting happens. His older daughter – the alpha girl – says something to the alpha boy. She and he do some pointing. She speaks to her little sister, who takes a toy over to the younger boy, and they position it on the prow of the boat. Within seconds, the four of them have begun an involved and interesting game featuring 'princesses, giants, treasure

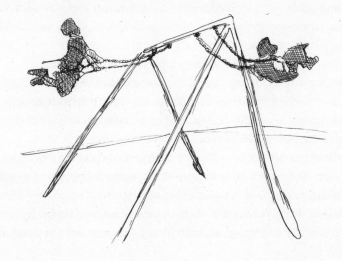

... and Cinderella's lost shoe'. It goes on for ages, and they have a great time.

The boys were not intentionally dominating, though that's not beyond boys to do by any means, they were just being energetic. It had a displacing effect on the girls, though. Left to themselves (that is, without adult intervention), the girls made their move, not to fight but to integrate with the boys, to not just 'share the space' but share their minds as well. A game developed that was more fun than either pair would have had, the girls' imaginations and the boys' passion blending in a way that bodes well for all their futures.

When Things Go Wrong

Parents only need to get involved when nothing else seems to work. A discussion with your child that begins with their tearful complaint that 'nobody will play with me' can lead to working out – well, how did it go wrong? You can talk to her about the 'sharing of importance' and letting others have some say in the game.

It can get very intense. One of the shocking things, to parents as well as to children themselves, is how rough and heartless kids can sometimes be. But it's simply that they haven't learned to mask their emotions. They can hate fiercely, but briefly, and then all is forgiven. We shouldn't get involved unless violence threatens or someone comes running to get us. Even when that happens, try to avoid taking sides, but give them a chance to chill out and recover their poise. They will usually bounce back, and the game will have moved on.

By late primary school, girls' friendships start to deepen into real emotional sharing. They will usually have one special friend, or perhaps a trio who get along well and are quite inseparable. The reason for this deepening of friendship in the pre- and early teens is that friends are part of the long journey away from depending just on Mum and Dad. As we become adults, we don't so much become independent, we just depend on a wider group of people.

In girls this is revealed in their sharing of secrets. Under-fives will tell everything to anyone, and can be very embarrassing at times, but from five to ten most children are intensely loyal to their families. In therapy, a girl of this age will rarely speak about her mother's drinking or her father's anger, for example. She needs her family so much that she feels drawn to protect them. But around the age of ten, girls begin to stand away from their family and see it in a clearer light. By mid-adolescence, girls will confide to a friend their deepest concerns and problems with their family. This can be a much-needed source of comfort and support since there is often some healthy and necessary conflict with parents at this time. Just as we comforted them about their friends, in primary school, *their friends comfort them about us* in secondary school.

Sharing problems is part of bonding – to such a degree that quite secure girls will make up problems ('OMG, my parents, they just *baby* me so much!') to be able to show empathy for a friend who has real stress in her family.

Primary school friends are for companionship and fun. In the teens you can add to this that they need their friends as a sounding board and for emotional support.

UNLIKELY FRIENDS

Sometimes girls will make unlikely friends. Play expert and psychologist Michael Thompson describes a classic case.[3] A fashionable and cool 12-year-old girl whose parents are going through a messy divorce makes friends with a studious and less sociable girl, who is steady and caring. Together they play games about cabins in the forest, horses and princesses. For the cool girl, it's a huge relief to be able to still be a child with a patient friend who doesn't care about fitting in, boys or clothes. Her fashionable friends are totally bewildered, but the differences enrich each girl and give them each a wider possibility of who they can be. Complementary friends – who are different in a way that balances the different strengths of each – offer much more than being with girls who are all the same. Even for a short time, they bring benefits and growth.

What Are the Skills of Friendship?

Once again, friendship skills all begin in babyhood. The secure attachment of mother and baby lays the foundations for being trusting, being available to love and to have a closeness with others. *If your daughter was close to you, she will know how to be close to others.*

The girls your daughter tries to befriend will sometimes be from insecurely attached babyhoods – mums who were cold and indifferent or stressed and depressed – and these friends may bring these 'issues' to their friendship role. An insecure girl may show this by being clingy and wanting to own and not ever share her newly made friend. Or she may be dominating and controlling – we have to *do what I say*, and *go where I choose*. Perhaps she will overcome this if a secure friendship manages to grow, but often our girls find these companions all too much and flee. If your daughter is the insecure one, it might be that she needs more closeness and friendship from you before she is ready to feel safe with others of her own age. Mothers and fathers are their daughter's first friends.

Check on your own behaviour – are you calm, grounded and available for your daughter when you are together? Some daughters need more reassurance than others. Some mums (or dads) are erratic – extravagantly overinvolved one minute, distracted the next. Their

daughters soon put up shields as this is just too hard to handle. But take heart, nobody is perfect, and just as with all her friendships, your relationship with your daughter is always an opportunity to learn how to iron out the bumps.

There are seven core skills involved in being a friend:

1. *Enjoying the company of others – lightening up and treating company as a chance for fun. Many a girl has started out shy, but with gentle encouragement has come out of her shell.*

2. *Learning to take turns and share – this means that you give up some of what you want for the pleasure of being with someone else. Point out to her that you have more fun if you play together, but you have to give a little to make that work.*

3. *Being able to empathise – imagining how you would feel in your friend's shoes, and being happy for them when they 'win' or 'star' in the game. This is a more advanced skill, one that doesn't always come easily.*

4. *Being able to regulate aggression – not screaming or clobbering your friends when you disagree. Not storming off because you are losing the argument.*

5. *Apologising when you are wrong, or have hurt a friend's feelings.*

6. *Being able to read emotions – seeing when someone is angry, sad or afraid and adjusting your behaviour accordingly. You can even teach this with drawings of smiley, frowny, teary and shaky faces, helping your daughter recognise them, and applying this to situations when her friends have been upset.*

7. *Learning when to trust or believe someone, and when not to, and understanding that people can be deceptive for reasons of their own. Your daughter will be shocked and hurt when a friend lies or deceives her. You will need to comfort her and explain that some people have not learned the value of being trustworthy. Don't lose heart, just be a little careful.*

Each of these issues will arise often in your daughter's day-to-day life. When she comes to you hurt or bewildered, you can pinpoint which skill is called for, listen to her feelings, but then talk to her about how that skill can be put into practice. It will take a few goes to get right, so follow up with her over a few days or weeks. Even we adults often don't get these situations right, so have respect for the hugeness of what she is having to learn, and praise and affirm her for even small steps.

THE SAME-AGE GHETTO

When talking about girls' friends we seem to automatically assume that means same-sex peers. We probably have school to blame for that, and also the disappearance of real community from the way we live. In the last 50 years girls have often been reduced to just the nuclear family, and their school classmates, for their social options, but this is actually quite unnatural. Girls ideally also need friends who are young women, half a generation older, savvy and yet youthful enough to relate to them with understanding. They need older women in their 60s and 70s too, grandmother figures, who offer a grounded, wise and comforting presence. They also need smaller or younger children who look up to them, get cuddles from them, and give them a taste of the joys of nurturing and being depended on, to relieve them of self-obsession and too much inwardness. They need boys or men friends who have no partnering or sexual intent towards them, so that they can expand out of those anxieties and see themselves as more completely human.

The chance to make these kinds of connections arise from the sort of street, town, or household you live in, the choices that you as her parents make with regards to the social and recreational life you lead. (A bland suburban life without belonging and participating can be crushingly isolating and impoverished for growing kids.) Belonging to a church, sporting group, community project or activist group exposes her to friendships with people who barely give a thought to weight, fashion or boys and yet are miraculously happy and alive! Daughters need to be among people who lift them up and need their contributions. This gives them a whole different kind of self-esteem.

Be a Friendship Role Model

As with most skills in life, a role model is the very best kind of help you can be. If a girl's mum goes up and talks to people in social settings, shows interest and chats animatedly with them, her daughter can see how it's done, and also how it creates a good feeling. A mum who is grumpy and doesn't have time for people is not likely to have a daughter who has those skills. If you are naturally shy, though, or she is, don't push it; the first step is to be comfortable with yourself. Often Dad has different social skills to Mum, and a daughter can mix and match what she observes in her parents and other close family members.

Sharing and taking turns is usually learned by having brothers and sisters. If your daughter is an only child, you might have to teach this and practise it at home. Helping your kids get along at home, patiently but dedicatedly, insisting on respect, kindness and sharing, and solving conflicts calmly, will greatly help them to transfer those skills to their wider lives at school and elsewhere. If she is rude to you, then she will be rude to others, who might be less tolerant. So working on respect will really benefit her.

Empathy is learned through the experience of others showing it to you. Use feeling words, let your expression match that of your daughter and try to sympathise with her – take time to hear where her heart is. You will see your daughter at a young age begin to do the same with her dollies and teddies, as she bandages them, comforts them, and so on. That's a good sign that she will be a caring friend in real life.

Your daughter's ability to speak up for her rights matters a lot. If you are able to stand up to people in shops or at home, and speak out when you are unhappy, she will learn how to do this. When she has trouble with friends at school, you can rehearse with her the sort of things she could say, and how to word her objections so that she can be direct and clear in her response to them.

If you are a gentle or quiet person, parenthood might call on you to be tougher. Watch the movie *Oranges and Sunshine* – the heroine of that film, social worker Margaret Humphreys, is a gentle soul who fights governments and church authorities for the rights of her clients because of the power of her empathy for them. You don't have to be big or loud to be strong, just be clear – and don't give up.

When conflict arises, between you and your partner, for example, notice if you get angry or loud. Your daughter needs to see how you can keep your cool in tense situations. If you lose it all the time, she might decide to be different. Or she might end up being just like you!

Finally, it's great to sit down with your daughter and talk about 'what makes a good friend'. Make a list of all the things she can think of. Write them down. Then you can ask:

- *Does she think* she *is a good friend?*
- *Who is the best friend she has ever had? Why?*
- *Has she got better as a friend as she has got older?*
- *What are her challenges in being a good friend?*

These are great things to raise her consciousness about.

Friends can be an enormous source of strength and wellbeing. The skill of strong close relationships is one of the most important things you can give your daughter. It's worth the time you spend talking and helping her. Long after you are gone, she will still be drawing on your kindness and patience in figuring it all out.

A COUNSELLOR TALKS ABOUT FRIENDSHIPS AND GIRLS

Johanna is a counsellor in the primary department of a big grammar school.

As a school counsellor, I am usually called on when girls' relationships go amiss. In primary school, this seems to peak in Year 4, but can sometimes hot up in Year 3 and continue in Year 5. It's good to put energy in at these times before it all revs up again in Year 8 and Year 9!

Sadly, isolation by exclusion, 'death stares', giggles and pointing are all everyday occurrences at school, usually because one or two of the girls are less happy in themselves and fall into these hurtful ways of behaving. All the girls need help to stand up to this, and not become part of the problem. It's important that meanness isn't just allowed to keep on happening or a happy environment can soon be lost.

What works?

Both preventively and as a response when things are getting a bit much, we have special get-togethers to discuss 'being friends'. We talk about what is the recipe for a good friendship, what do we offer in a friendship, that we are all different, but all want to feel included and cared for.

These small circle groups are run by teachers sensitive to girls' relational dynamics (and who don't just write it all off as 'girls' stuff'). Mean behaviour needs to be directly discussed so that it's out in the open, and they know strategies to interrupt bullying or stop silly acts of hurt from happening.

Adults need to know and be part of what is going on with girls and their peers. We shouldn't say 'that's their world' because it's unnatural for kids of the same age to be left to work it out for themselves, and it usually doesn't work.

Emily – Be My Shadow or Else!

Emily, 8, doesn't want her friend Anna to play with anyone else but her. She accuses Anna of not really being her friend if she wants to play with someone else. Anna is anxious about telling Emily that she likes football and playing with a big group of children. She fears losing a friendship that she does enjoy for the most part.

What works?

Putting the question: How can we make sure that everyone's needs are being met?

The girls, if given support to work through this, do come up with the answers and a good plan. In this case, the girls devised a roster that on Mondays and Wednesdays Anna would play football in a big group and Emily and the other girls would understand that they weren't being rejected and that Anna still valued their friendship. On Tuesday and Thursday, Emily and Anna would spend time together playing handball.

Maya – The Unappreciated Matchmaker

In order to try and gain popularity, Maya, 10, spends her lunchtime running between groups of boys and girls discussing who likes who and telling the rest of the class that this girl and that boy are girlfriend and boyfriend. The girl involved is mortified by this attention. She starts to not come to school some days. Eventually her mother finds out the problem and talks to the class teacher. The teacher explains to the class that Year 5 is too early for girlfriends and boyfriends and it's better to focus on friendships in general.

What works?

The school counsellor met with Maya. Through sensitive discussion it emerged that Maya feels lonely at school and has difficulties maintaining friendships. She thought that this would be a way of being accepted by the other girls. They started to look at other ways of developing and maintaining friendships that would be more successful.

Alpha Girls

In any school there is usually a group of alpha girls who are more confident and vocal. The other girls in the class tend to be more thoughtful and kind, and prefer to observe the world before jumping in with both boots. If teachers are not aware and connected to this dynamic, the alpha girls dominate, get the best classroom jobs, the star roles in plays and lobby the teacher for their preferred way of things to happen. They can make the other girls miserable and have unfair influence and power.

It is important that the teachers even the playing field, and make sure that things are equitable and no one is left out. They need to rotate roles and responsibilities and have activities that value different things – such as being careful, quiet or slow, as well as dazzlingly talented! Not everyone wants to be an alpha girl, but everyone wants things to be fair.

How Feelings Work

Feelings or emotions (we use the words interchangeably) are a compass for being around other people. We need to have two sets of skills: firstly, to read our own feelings and listen to what they are telling us; secondly, to read other people's feelings, so we know how to treat them, care for them, or even stay away from them.

If you understand the language of feelings, you can better pass on this knowledge to your daughter and make her confident and strong.

Humans have hundreds of different feelings, but the main social ones are simple and easy. There are only four: *fear, sadness, anger and joy.* These four 'points of the compass' help us to know how to take care of ourselves:

> *when we feel afraid we get cautious;*
> *when we are angry we stand up for ourselves;*
> *when we are sad, we go inwards and reflect, and may want to hold*
> *   or be held by someone we feel safe with;*
> *when we feel joy, we relax and celebrate and restore our spirits.*

These four feelings can mix and match like the colours we blend to get every shade of the rainbow, but usually deep down we have one feeling at a time, and it really helps to be able to know what it is, in ourselves and in others.

Most living creatures have feelings: bees get angry; fish know fear and dart away from danger; further up the line, elephants and great apes grieve and mourn. We human beings have the most sophisticated and complex emotions, but they are still based on those basic four listed above.

Emotions are a strong 'guidance system', like a GPS, that you can use to understand and help your child. Ask yourself 'what are they feeling?' (What does that expression, that action, those words, tell me about their inner state?) Ask them about their feelings, get them to name them, and let them tell you what is going on in their world. This can lead to uncovering the causes of those feelings, if you are patient and win their trust, and to talking through what to do. But the feelings always need to come first, and sometimes your daughter won't want anything more than to get it off her chest and she will feel better again.

Fear – And Listening to Your Intuition

Many years ago in the United States a serial killer was finally caught after taking the lives of numerous young women. After his capture the police made an amazing discovery – that dozens of girls had encountered him *but not gone with him.* Asked why, they said 'I had a bad feeling about it' or even, 'I don't know, I just felt something wasn't right'. *These girls listened to their body signals.* They were saved by listening to their fear.

Most girls are naturally helpful and compassionate. People wanting to exploit or hurt them may try to play on their sympathy by telling them, 'I am looking for my lost dog', or 'I am feeling ill, can you help me?'

Listening to your own feelings and inner voice, and trusting it, is a 'strong woman' skill. Tell your daughter that she has this inner voice, and teach her how to listen to it. Share examples from your own life.

See if she can think of instances when she has heard that voice and it has taught her something.

GIRLS AND ASPERGER'S

Somebody who is disabled at reading or knowing feelings (such as someone with Asperger Syndrome or a degree of autism) may find other people totally bewildering. They will keep talking to someone who is totally bored, or be friendly and gushing with a complete stranger. They may not realise that someone, such as their own mother or sibling, is sad when it would be totally obvious to even a stranger.

Girls with Asperger's use more of their brain to think through this, and so are less often diagnosed than boys – boys have more trouble hiding the problem.

Asperger's can range from slight to full-blown, so watch for signs that your daughter finds people bewildering and upsetting and just can't figure out what to do right, such as if she is inordinately anxious in situations that don't seem to warrant it, or she seems forced and artificial in relating to people, when you know she is doing her best.

The solution is the same as with a girl who isn't on the autistic spectrum; to help her learn the language of emotion, and by logic and gradual experience learn to be comfortable socially. It just might take more support and explicit explaining of things that other children might naturally know. Fortunately, children with Asperger's are often very intelligent and can bring their 'computer' brain to bear on the situation. They can think logically about what to do and say in social situations, and how to read others' feelings. In fact, they sometimes become more sensitive and connected than people who merely do this on autopilot. Don't be shy to seek out professional advice about help and training for her to learn good strategies.

A SECRET WORD

From the age of five, sometimes your daughter will go to someone's house and be away from your immediate protection. You need to know she is safe. One strategy is to have a 'secret word' or phrase that she can use when she rings you, one that lets you know she doesn't feel right, or that something is making her uncomfortable. You and she can memorise this word and its use, very seriously, for whenever it's needed. For instance, she can ask to phone you and say 'my shoes are hurting', or 'I saw an eagle today' (a code word you make up together is best) which means 'Please come and get me straight away'.

You will probably never need this secret word, but if you do, it's very helpful. Even discussing this alerts her to the idea that some places and people don't feel right, and if you notice that, we will always rescue you.

It's a fine balance; you don't want to make her afraid of the world outside your door, just alert in the way that kids are all over the world in more uncertain environments.

Teach her in a calm, strong way, and give examples in day-to-day life: 'that person smiled with their mouth but not with their eyes'. Girls can be observant and aware that people have all kinds of different motives, and if they don't feel right, they should get away fast.

Anger Is About Being Strong

Anger is also part of our protective system. Used properly, anger does not mean shouting, hitting people or acting abusively, but instead is a strengthening feeling that you won't be pushed around. If your daughter reads the signs in her body – a heating up and tensing of muscles, clenching of jaw muscles, or a frowning feeling in her face – then she knows '*I am being made to do something I don't really want*', or 'These people are saying or doing things just to be mean, I won't let them get to me.'

The quickest and best use of anger is to voice it. Teach your daughter to say 'I don't like that' in a strong voice, to glare, and stick her chin out: 'Leave me alone', or to walk away while staring at the person who has insulted her or hurt her. Actually practise this with her, coach her to look and sound tough. If it's a friend she is feeling annoyed with, she can say 'I don't want to do that', or 'No, I won't' more gently, but meaning it, and perhaps having to repeat herself a couple of times – 'I've said how I feel.' Of course, if you too sometimes model these behaviours, she will simply imitate you when the need arises.

When our daughter started at pre-school, the teacher told us that she was the only girl who would play with the boys. We were proud of her because it showed she was adaptable and adventurous. We weren't sure what her secret was to enjoying the rough and tumble way the boys played, but on more than one occasion, walking from the car park to the leafy outdoor play area attached to the school, we heard her voice loud and clear: 'I don't like that!' She was comfortable around the boys, because she knew how to set them straight!

Sadness Is Real

Sadness is a quieter and more inward feeling. It is about making changes on the inside, whereas fear and anger are about doing things on the outside. When we feel sad, our primary need is to be understood. Comfort, the time to express it, gives your girl the space to let go of the loss or disappointment. Often as parents we can't bear for our kids to be sad, and we try to rush them out of it with food treats or attempts at humour. It is better to trust that sadness will pass if we stay connected and give it time.

There are often things in a girl's day that might make her sad; a friend has let her down at school, someone she likes is moving away, a teacher promises something but does not deliver, they see an animal dead on the road, or something awful on a newsflash and it tears at their heart. We can't fix these things, we just gradually find a sense of perspective, and your daughter will have to make this journey, too, it is years long and you can't rush it.

The world IS a sad place, and children can cope with this if their feelings are simply allowed to be, while we stay close by, sending the signal, 'yes, but you don't have to bear it on your own'.

Joy

Joy is something that we need to cultivate and celebrate. In other cultures, people know a happy moment when they see one, and grab it with both hands. Everybody's in the kitchen just hanging around? Turn up the music and dance. Pick your child up and twirl them around if you feel like it. Hug often. Lie about in a blissful heap with your children on the couch. Be silly when out in the open. 'Horse around' in parks and on beaches. Smooch your child or tickle them mercilessly when the impulse takes you. Buy ice cream. Sing in the car.

Celebrate events. Don't go in for lots of presents, go in for simple memorable good times. At Christmas, enjoy your extended family, and remember that there really IS peace on Earth for 95 per cent of the human race.

Teach your daughter to laugh, to dance, to be wild and free, so her capacity for joy expands and develops. It's the antidote to the necessary suffering that is also a part of life, and it ensures that happiness has a permanent place in her soul.

Tend and Befriend

At the heart of our understanding of babies is a concept called 'attachment'. This is the scientific name for the bond between mother and baby. Some babies attach securely to their mums, some do not. These patterns tend to persist into adult life – if we don't learn how to love as a baby, we might have trouble loving as an adult. Over about 60 years of attachment research, though, nobody had asked the gender question: is it different for boys and girls?

When they did, something surprising was found.[4] Boys who were insecurely attached would avoid their mothers or not trust them. This was simple self-protection: 'she's not there for me, so I won't invest my feelings in her'. However, many of the girls responded differently. When their mother was depressed or distant or even when she was angry, these girls, barely out of babyhood, would *go closer to their mother and try to comfort her!*

On the one hand, this might seem very cute, and has survival value if the mother can revive her spirits, but it also has long-term risks. When in danger or conflict, most people respond with what is called a 'fight or flight' reaction, filling with adrenaline and preparing to get out of danger. Insecurely attached girls, though, had a 'tend and befriend' reaction; they too were very anxious, but they did not go away from danger, *they went towards it.* There is a very important consequence of this, while well-loved children are attracted to peaceful, caring and warm friends and partners, girls with 'tend and befriend' patterns will feel most comfortable around angry/depressed people, who unconsciously remind them of mum. These girls will have a strong belief system that it's their job to choose someone with mood swings, or violent tendencies, and try to fix them. I don't have to spell out what a problem this can become.

'Tend and befriend' skills have their advantages. In the workplace, women managers are far more likely to sidestep a potential conflict, see someone's aggression as just anxiety, and empathically listen to all sides of a problem. It's a brilliant skill that can bring about world peace as well as happy families. We badly need more of this, and for men to learn it too, but it has to be a conscious choice, not a compulsion – if it's an unconscious pattern in intimate relationships, it can lead to harm.

If you have a daughter who is always a peacemaker, do affirm and value that, but make sure she can also mobilise some anger when needed, can stand up for herself, and doesn't get used by her friends. If you notice your daughter being too much like this, encourage her to ask 'what do I want myself?' and be just a little more assertive.

AVOIDING DUD FRIENDS

Your daughter will sometimes benefit from some direct advice about spotting and avoiding dodgy friends. For example …

Notice if you are changing yourself in order to keep a friend. Doing things that you don't really like, that are not you, because it's what they want. If you do this at the start of a friendship, you may find you have to keep it up to keep them. It's probably not worth it, and better to not start. A real friend is someone who is happy to compromise or take turns.

Sometimes you can make a friend who is chronically crabby. You assume it's because of something you have done wrong, and find yourself often 'dancing around' trying to fix it. A chronically crabby (cc) person is sometimes just made that way – it's their approach to life, it rarely changes, and it gets a lot of control. You will just end up being exhausted, so find happy friends instead.

GIRLS AND SPORT

Sport is good for girls. It's social, it's physical, it builds confidence, it allows them to let off steam. Sport is a celebration of our body's capacities, and it also increases and strengthens those capacities. It's a vital part of healthy girlhood. There is a vast choice now in what you can play and do.

Pre-School Age
Under the age of five, the very best sport is to simply play. Go to places where they can run around; have outings to the park, countryside or the beach with friends or just picnics in the garden so that there is more encouragement to be active and play games. Organised sport for littlies like toddler gym or ballet need to be checked out carefully because structured classes invite comparison and pressure when the girls are way too young. Sometimes these classes are run in a fun way but, in general, informal natural play opportunities are best.

Playgroups are an ideal part of a toddler's week because mums, dads and kids can all find company and get new skills in a fun environment that is unpressured and inexpensive.

Before Adolescence
Under the age of ten, girls are very open to sport as they have not yet become too self-conscious to enjoy themselves. They are also equal in ability to boys, if not better coordinated. The more different sports pre-adolescent girls take part in, the better, as this helps muscle, bone and posture development across all their body areas. It's also more fun.

Swimming and climbing are good for upper body development, balance is helped by dance, skating, or court sports, and team sports involve aerobic exercise and lower body strength. Some girls love the fun and excitement of a team sport and its bonding friendships. But if your daughter really doesn't like team sports, there are lots more individual ones she could try, such as athletics or weights; and creative options like dance, yoga or gymnastics that can still give her joy in her body.

By getting some skill in lots of sports, your daughter has the most choice of enjoyable recreation being available when she is a student or young adult. Fun is the aim – watch out for coaches who are anxious or performance driven and who pass this pressure on to the kids. Pressure leads to injuries, because children are forced to move out of their natural grace and pleasure in moving about and strain themselves. Choose sports and coaches who are warm and see the sport as something for the kids, not the other way round. At this age, you want her to enjoy what she does, that way she will want to keep doing it when she is older.

In Adolescence

From ten upwards, there are challenges getting some girls to play sport. It helps if the foundations have been laid by lots of interest (perhaps especially from dads) in the earlier years, but still even very sporting girls suddenly don't want to play, and won't say why. Often it's about feeling self-conscious – we have made girls so uptight about looking perfect, and in sport you are more aware of the differences between body shapes and sizes, and there is an uncoordinated phase around the age of 13 when our arms and legs don't seem to do what we want due to brain reorganisation.

Worst of all, many girls diet at this age. This is the worst possible time for them to do this as their increased growth rate through adolescence means there's a huge need for calcium (at least 1200mg a day) and energy, as well as vitamins and other minerals, especially iron for menstruating girls. Exercising your body builds the bone strength that you will depend on sixty years later when osteoporosis threatens. Bones grow if you use them, at this age, like at no other time.

So this is the time to help your daughter find one or two sports that she really enjoys. Remove all obstacles to her playing them, and perhaps get involved as an adult in the transport or coaching so that you can be with her and also support her friends in that sport, as this is an age at which kids appreciate more than just Mum and Dad to talk to and learn from.

The opposite risk – obsessive over-emphasis on a sport – is also there, as girls in their teens are capable of losing all sense of perspective. Be sure to check that your super-athletic daughter has days off, doesn't train to her detriment, and still eats well and in a relaxed way. Be physical for fun – go to the beach or play netball in the garden, don't let it all be about competition. Some years ago there was an Australian Senate Inquiry into abusive training levels in the national gymnastic team – girls were having delayed puberty and were not menstruating until their twenties because of the huge stress put on their bodies through training when they were still so young. This would likely have permanent and damaging effects. It's all about balance!

If your daughter just doesn't like sport, look for activities like dancing, hiking, boogie boarding, kayaking or fishing which are individual and non-competitive but still take joy in movement and being in the physical world. It can be hard if she is shy or just would rather be playing The Sims or Left for Dead on a computer, but don't give up trying to find ways she can find joy in her body.

Keep sport fun, sociable and without too much pressure to win. Make sure the adult mentors are healthy and balanced people, and if they are not, change to a different team or a different sport. Get involved, too, so that you can get to know and care about her friends, who perhaps won't all have parents who are so good hearted.

WHAT HAPPENS IN PUBERTY?

Puberty in girls starts on average at about age 10, but it's incredibly variable – it can be any time between eight and 16! It's important to prepare your daughter for this phase so she has a positive attitude and feels informed and grown-up about it.

Breasts
The first sign of puberty for most girls is breast budding. Usually this becomes apparent as a firm tender lump under the nipple of one or both breasts. Within six months, this is usually on both sides and spreading wider than the 'areola' (the dark area round the nipple). After another twelve months the breast usually has grown to something like its mature size and shape.

But breast development is incredibly variable, and it's important to explain this to your girl. Being the first in your class to have breasts can cause embarrassment, and breasts arriving a bit late may worry some girls, especially in our sexualised environment when such things are made into a bigger deal than they should be.

Pubic Hair
Within a couple of months of breast changes beginning, pubic hair starts to grow, at first around the labia (lips) of the vagina and later spreading up to the mound around her lower abdomen. In about 15 per cent of girls, though, pubic hair starts growing before breasts start to bud. Everyone is different.

Menstruation
Usually about two years after the start of breast budding, or around age 12 in most girls, the first menstrual bleeding happens. This is so variable, though, that you should tell your daughter about it long before you suspect it might happen, just to be on the safe side. Remember, some girls can start their periods as early as eight. (We still hear of girls finding blood on their knickers and not knowing what is

wrong, being terrified that they have something wrong, or deeply embarrassed because nobody prepared them.)

You can tell her about pads; she may already be familiar with you talking about periods and managing them, and if you have a positive attitude that really helps. Rather than seeing menstruation as just a nuisance, focus on the big picture that this is a great sign of growing up, and being able to one day have babies if she chooses. Remind her that having her periods shouldn't stop her doing almost anything she wants. Be happy for her, and she will catch that spirit. Let her carry a slim pad in her purse or bag in case she needs it, and let her know that she can also ask the nurse at school in an 'emergency'.

In the first few years periods are not regular. They can come at any time.

Ovulation (where an egg is released and she can get pregnant) doesn't always happen with early periods, it may take several years before a girl ovulates on *every* cycle, but you can't rely on that. You, and she, need to know that pregnancy is now a possibility.

Hips

Girls will get more chubby about 18 months before puberty begins – usually around age eight or nine. This is often the first sign of puberty being on its way. As the oestrogen levels in her body rise, her hips and pelvis will widen (to make it easier for babies to be born). She will often have a growth spurt and become much taller, too, at this time, becoming close to her adult final height.

Other Stuff

Vaginas clean themselves, and sometimes a whitish secretion comes from a girl's vagina once puberty has begun. Tell your daughter about this too, and that it's healthy and normal.

Skin gets a lot oilier in puberty, which can be a bit of a pain. Pimples and acne are more common, and also you sweat much more. Help your daughter find natural and healthy ways to manage this – stay away from chemicals or harsh treatments if you can.

Celebrate

Don't make puberty sound like a big negative, it's really important to convey the excitement and amazement of being a woman. Some people have a special mother, aunties, grandmas and daughter grown-up dinner, or go camping together or to a nice hotel. Some people devise rituals or sharing times for their daughter with the women who love her. Celebrate. This is a time for honouring and appreciating your daughter's success in growing up well.

GIRLS JOURNEYING TOGETHER: GIRLS' GROUPS FOR THE YEAR OF GROWING UP

Just occasionally, an innovation happens which makes you think 'Wow! That is so needed, so obvious, and so great, why didn't anyone think of it before?'. Girls Journeying Together groups are one of those ideas. Devised by Kim McCabe, a specialist in girls' education, these groups have been quietly taking hold in England and seem set to spread all over the world.

The idea is simple. Girls Journeying Together groups are a programme of half-day sessions, held once a month over a whole year. They are for girls as they enter puberty, who undergo 'a journey of curiosity about what lies ahead'. With a well-trained and experienced woman leader, but also drawing on their mothers and other key women in their lives for support, the groups (at most 12 girls) discuss the ups and downs of adolescence, peer pressure, social media, relating to boys (and girls), social life, school and family. And what becoming a women means to them.

This is a group away from your normal friends, where the rules are very different. Uppermost among the principles is one that really touched me deeply to hear about, and will do so for most parents, or anyone who remembers being a young person. YOU DON'T HAVE TO 'FIT IN'. This single most liberating guideline, as it begins to be explored, sets the girls free from the endless and harrowing experience many have of walking a tightrope of conformity with what others think they should do, be and think.

Girls just love these groups. At this age, they want to understand what's happening as their bodies develop, their moods fluctuate and their relationships change. They want reassurance that all is still well. Older women can give them this reassurance. Girls also want to know that they're not alone. The camaraderie that grows over the year shows them the strength that comes from true friends. When the year is over, many of these kids remain friends for life.

Girls (usually in their final year of primary school) come to a trial session so each can decide if she wants to be part of the group. The mothers don't just drop their daughters off once a month, they also meet to discuss topics that dovetail with what the girls are covering and to form a circle of support around the girls. Halfway through they join the girls' group for a session of sharing experiences and affirming the girls. At the end of the year the mothers are invited to join their daughters for a ceremonial celebration. The group of girls are full of affection for one another and feel so much better prepared for all that lies ahead. The mothers too. The support then continues twice a year right through the girls' teen years.

Did you enter your teens feeling like there was someone you could talk to about everything that was changing inside you? Did you have a group of friends who you felt safe to be yourself with because they accepted you just as you were? Belonging to a Girls Journeying Together group during puberty can be enormously supportive to mothers and daughters alike.

Each girl is encouraged to be herself, to dress and speak and behave true to however she is that day. They learn how to accept each other and experience feeling accepted by a group of peers.

Girls in a Girls Journeying Together group will:

- learn about the changes that puberty brings
- discuss the influences of peers, media, culture, and parents
- prepare for their own first period and support one another
- get to know each other really well – well enough to dare to speak their innermost fears and heartfelt hopes
- dream into their futures
- clarify their values
- (only when the time is right) talk of dating, diets, drinking, exams and other teenage concerns
- laugh and cry and play and feast
- find mentors
- and in time become mentors themselves.

Anxiety about what lies ahead turns into assurance and anticipation. Girls are guided into adulthood with a real opportunity of avoiding many of the mental health issues that are so prevalent today. They have fun and make friends while learning what they need to know to grow up strong and free.

I am hopeful that these groups are one day available in every community, for every girl. For details of the groups, facilitation training, and any other information, go to www.ritesforgirls.com.

In a Nutshell

- Friends are really important to girls.
- Between five and ten social skills are being learned big time.
- There are seven key skills: friendliness, sharing, empathy, controlling aggression, apologizing, reading emotions and knowing who to trust. She will need help to learn these.
- She will learn by copying you too.
- Each of the four emotions (anger, fear, sorrow and joy) has a purpose to guide her.
- 'Tend and befriend' is a useful skill but it can get out of control. Sometimes you need 'fight or flight'.
- Sport can be great, especially if you can find the right one for your girl.
- Understand about puberty and prepare your daughter well in advance – by about the age of eight!
- Girls' puberty support groups are a new innovation that can really help.

Chapter 5

Finding Her Soul

(10–14 years)

Often by late primary school girls can seem very grown-up, sensible and mature.

Parents heave a sigh of relief and wonder if that's the job done. Of course, as everyone knows, this is just the lull before the storm! Soon, the hormonal rockets fire up, and the next adventure begins. The timing of puberty varies greatly, as we've mentioned, but whenever it comes, it has a profound effect. Up until now, most girls have been unself-conscious, rambunctious kids who live happily for today. They ride, swim, make a noise, play sport, get involved in creative activities, and generally breeze through life. Their confidence and can-do attitude make them a joy to be around.

Puberty doesn't necessarily change this, but it adds a new 'inwardness' to a girl's nature. She senses adulthood is coming towards her, and prompted by those unmistakable signals she can't help but start to think about the kind of woman she is to become. There is excitement, as well as fear, and even sadness at the loss of childhood freedom and simplicity. This often makes her more reflective and somewhat more private. Observant dads and mums will notice this distinct change of 'season' in their daughter. A girl at this age starts to ask herself, 'who am I?', 'what do I want?' and 'what is my life really about?'. Her answers to these questions will guide her choices through the next decade of her life.

Take every chance she gives you, on car trips or while doing tasks together, or as you sit with her in her room at bedtime, to listen to what she says and to ask her about her thoughts about her life and her world. You will find you start to share more about your own life, your teen experiences, your beliefs and ideas, and that she is now more ready to listen. Suddenly you are not so distant in age.

Preparation Begins in Earnest

The years from 10 to 14 are far more important than most people real-ise – they are not something to skip over. This is a time of intense prepa-ration. We have to help girls to stay in this place and not to rush into premature attempts at being grown-up, for which they are far from ready. If you take nothing else from this chapter, or even this whole book, please take this: girls from 10 to 14 years old need more, not less, of our time, interest and *availability*. This is when we ramp up our teaching, explaining, coaching, enquiring, and when we involve her in more demanding activity, preparing her to be the amazing woman she can become. But we don't push her out there alone yet, or let the world grab her with its pressures to conform, compete, be sexual or please boys in order to feel okay. She is preparing for womanhood, but that preparation is a stage all of its own.

Spark

Between 10 and 14, a girl's job is to get her roots down deep into who she is. There are many ways to do this. The first, and easiest, is called 'spark' ...

Dr Peter Benson, who died tragically young in 2011, was founder of the Search Institute in the US and one of the world's leading experts on adolescence. Peter spent the final years of his life campaigning for one single idea that he felt could transform the quality of both home and school life for young people – the idea that we all have a '*spark*'.[1]

When parents are asked what are their aspirations for their daugh-ters they hardly ever say things like, 'To make our nation more interna-tionally competitive' or, 'To get high scores on the NAPLAN testing at Year 12'. (So sorry, politicians, you have missed the point altogether.) Parents say, 'I want her to love life' or, 'I want her to be kind and compassionate' or, 'I want her to find her passion in life and follow it'. We love our kids, and so our goals for them are founded in that: we want them to find deep satisfaction in their hearts.

The question is, how? Peter Benson discovered something which seems so simple, but it is a complete game-changer. He discovered that children and young teenagers almost always have something inside them – an interest, enthusiasm, talent or concern – which, *if it is supported, gives them incredible joy, motivation and direction.* That thing is their *spark*.

His studies found the following remarkable facts.

1. *Asked the question 'What activity gives you the most joy, makes you feel most alive, gives you a sense of purpose and excitement?' 100 per cent of children understood the idea.*
2. *About 65 per cent of all kids could tell you at least one activity that filled those criteria for them. They knew what their spark was.*
3. *Another 20 per cent, when prompted by an adult who knew them, could also find their spark (they were just too shy to say so straight out).*
4. *Of these children, 10 per cent had more than one thing that sparked them. Lucky kids!*

Benson loved to quote the ancient philosopher Plutarch who said: 'the young are not vessels to be filled, they are fires to be lit.' Those teachers who understand this are the ones who are loved by kids and appreciated by parents.

How About Your Daughter?

Does your daughter have a spark? Do you know what it is? Is her spark alight, or is it going out? What would it take to see it really burning bright?

The key to your daughter finding herself, and beginning to really blossom as a person, at age 10 to 14 (or younger), might be as simple as this, ask her 'What do you really love to do?', then, 'How can I help you to do that?' 'What are the obstacles to doing it that I can help you overcome?' 'Who else do we need to get on board (at school, or in the community) to be able to do that?'

To help parents with this spark-chasing, Benson separated sparks into three kinds:

1. ***A skill or talent*** *– for instance, to draw, write, be athletic, dance or make music. Your child is just naturally good at this, and she enjoys doing it greatly.*
2. ***A commitment*** *– for example to protect the natural world, to work for social justice. It's the power of their caring that powers them along.*
3. ***A quality of character*** *– a part of their personality, such as empathy – being the one who others go to talk to. Or courage – being the one who speaks up or takes the lead to get something fixed up. (If something is happening, you can bet it will be your child out at the front!)*

Benson believes our job is to confirm and strengthen our child's spark. To blow on it, and help it ignite. 'If you discover a kid's spark, tell it back to them, tell them you see and hear it, thank them for possessing it. In almost all cases it's good, beautiful and useful to the world'. Of course, identifying her spark is just the beginning of some serious work for you as her parent to enable it to start to burn. But what could be more worthwhile?

Not All Sparks Are Kept Alive

It's here that Benson points out a tragic thing, and it was this that became his life's mission. *Only about a quarter of the young people* he studied were truly thriving in their lives – happy, engaged and with a strong sense of where they were going. He believed this was in most cases because the adults in their lives had not kept those kids' sparks alive, or even found out what they were.

He believed that there are *three critical things* that are required in a young girl if her spark is to burn brightly.

1. *There must be an adult* in her family *who gets behind her.*
2. *She also needs an adult* outside *the family – at school or in the community – who recognises and helps her.*
3. *There has to be the* opportunity *to encourage her spark and carry out whatever it needs to be lit.*

How many of us as adults had an interest that our parents couldn't be bothered to support? Or perhaps our parents were positive, but nobody at school cared, or there just wasn't a way in the community we lived in to follow that interest. How many millions of sparks just went out for lack of those ingredients? Surely we can do it differently?

Why It Matters

Why bother? What does it really matter? Peter Benson's research indicates that this discovery of an enthusiasm (and the support to follow it) affects some very important benchmarks. Children with sparks do better at school; they are happier and more confident, they engage better with adults, they get into less trouble either with their health and wellbeing, or with the law or school. (We shouldn't really need these other reasons to want our kids to be happy, but there they are.)

Your daughter's spark may change through life. We as adults know that sometimes we move on from one thing to another, but we take with us the sense of focus, application, self-belief and creativity. But equally often these sparks give us pleasure for life. A spark may become

our career, or it may not, but it is definitely at the heart of who we are. Your spark is your way of being in the world – artist, creator, writer, athlete, leader, carer, inventor, mystic, activist – this is your deep self, and that fire will keep you alive and sparking until the end of your days.

Actions You Can Take ...

Knowing your child's spark is a priority of a parent of a young teenager. It will help if you can remember your own spark history. What did you love to do as a child? Did it stay the same or change? Did your spark go out? What sparks your life now?

Discussing a child's spark should be part of every parent–teacher meeting. Schools should know the children's sparks and should help you find ways to encourage them.

Community groups, recreation departments or local councils should conduct surveys of the sparks that local children have and plan to provide those facilities and services to make sure they are encouraged.

A DIFFERENT GROUP OF FRIENDS

There is another reason why an activity or interest enriches or strengthens a girl, it provides her with an alternative *reference group* that may give her a much larger and more positive view of herself.

Often girls are trapped with only one friendship group – the accidental assemblage of same-age girls they meet at school. Apart from home (which also has its ups and downs) they have *no other view of themselves.* A girl can easily find her spirits sinking dangerously low because her peer group is too negative or destructive, but an interest group may be much more her kind of people. Also there may be mixed ages with all the benefits this brings. Interesting wise old men, feisty and eccentric women, friends from other schools or suburbs who are much more on her maturity level or share her interests. This gives her a different mirror in which she can see herself.

There are astonishing ranges of interests available to young girls, from Latin dance to rock climbing, quilting to scuba diving. There are hundreds of ways in which they can volunteer and be useful. Think outside the square of prepackaged activities that girls are 'supposed' to do, and instead consider things that people in the adult world pursue with passion. Don't merely crowd her life with multiple classes or activities after school, instead help her to search for just that kind of group where she feels really at home, and support her in letting that blossom.

A PLACE TO MAKE AND DO

If I could organise it, every girl would have a place to make and do – a kind of workshop/craft room, or corner of the house, peacefully away from TV sounds or smaller children, where messes could be left and projects take shape amongst endless materials, paints, tools, and so on. 'Making' – the creation of beautiful things – has emerged in recent years as a rediscovered expression of individuality, a way to be serene and an answer to the consumer madness in which girls express themselves merely by what they buy. Sculpture, painting, pottery, self-created fashion, art and craft of any kind seem to have a strengthening and healing effect on both boys and girls. Having a 'women's space' in the house that is sacrosanct and their own, just as men love their sheds, would be ideal.

Since few of us have houses that allow dedicated space, another option is just a roll-top desk or a corner that is her own place – not for schoolwork but for a freely chosen creativity.

Some communities around the world have begun to set up girls' and women's spaces – this might just be a weekly event in a borrowed room or hall where older women make teenage girls welcome in circles of creativity and earthy talk, and girls who are sometimes bordering on becoming street kids find a haven and a shoulder to lean on. Just as there are huge mental health benefits in the MensSheds movement (which may look like a surrender to stereotypes but in practice feels like liberation), women's spaces where older women teach and hang out with younger women would probably thrive in any community.

All That You Have Is Your Soul

When my wife was a trainee nurse in the 1970s, aged just 17, sometimes a patient would die. Shaaron would fetch the matron of the small country hospital, who would come into the room and do a rather strange thing – she would open the window just a crack. This was to let that person's soul leave. This is not what I mean here by soul (though I am not making fun of that idea, and perhaps they are related). When Tracey Chapman sang 'All That You Have Is Your Soul' she was talking about the deep-down essence of a person – who they really are, and what matters most to them. Soul is a hard thing to express in words, but everyone knows when a person has it. Some quite young people have soul, though it tends to come with experience, especially hard experience. Some folks clearly have none at all. They are selfish, shallow, anxious and grasping. They blow about in the slightest breeze. A person with soul is like a tree with deep roots, steady in the gale.

Watch a 10-year-old girl closely and you will see her starting to grow deeper roots. She dreams dreams that are her own private and fragile longings, which are not for sharing with other people. She asks big questions, and she watches the adults around her for clues as to how to live.

It's a good idea to think about the women you most like and admire. You'll find there is something that sets them apart – they are their own person. They have a kind of inner light. But it's not mystical – it comes from the fact that their lives add up. They have thought a long time about what really matters to them and they live in accordance with that. My favourite recent example is the New Zealand Prime Minister

Jacinda Ardern. Among the politicians we are used to (pale, male and stale!), she seems a whole lot more alive, but also more intelligent and principled. She wants to make national policy based on kindness and compassion.

Angela Merkel, the German Chancellor, is very different in style, but has the same ring of truth. You don't mess with her. But she cares about straight talking and doing the right thing. Politics is my enthusiasm but you will have your own idea of who is an admirable woman. Keep that in mind as you talk to your daughter, share with her your own ideas and express your own values.

Soul is a place inside you where you know what's right and what's wrong. While everybody has this place inside them, not everybody has travelled there. It needs people around us to gently, sincerely, nudge us to find it. Sometimes poetry helps, or a movie or a song. When her favourite auntie takes a girl out and in a quiet moment asks, 'What do you really want to do with your life?', it invites a girl into her soul. Nobody gives you soul, although they can show you theirs.

Soul means knowing yourself. If you break your own rules, nobody else will know, but you will hate yourself until you put things right. Soul is creative, it draws you to unique and special pathways, activities, means of expressing yourself. Soul is the real you. You can pretend to be someone else – *some people do that all their lives*. Many women through history have hidden their real selves away, and had a kind of suffocation of the spirit as a result. When you are being true to yourself, it feels right, even if nobody around you even *begins* to understand.

Daughters need this quality, at the ordinary everyday level as well as the lifetime level. When they fight with friends, or decide what to do or where to go, when a friend is getting drunk and wants them to be drunk too, or some boys ask them to pile into a car late at night, or her friends are being horrible to another girl at school. When she sees that her body in the mirror is a different shape to the airbrushed and photo-shopped bodies in the magazines, her soul whispers to her: 'I am me, and I am beautiful as I am.'

When she chooses what to study, who to be friends with, what career to follow, who to date or marry, the voice of her soul is the one she should listen to.

What Works for Developing Soul?

One way in which you can help your daughter develop soul is by *finding the right people* to bring into her life. Many people can be role models for your daughter, and show her how to be a strong, deep woman. These women include teachers both at school and in the special interests she may have, such as music, art or yoga, or perhaps some special sports coaches; young women in their twenties or thirties who help on camps and retreats, old people who love having girls at their house, aunts or grandmothers who have lived rich and interesting lives. All have their own *interiority* (a quiet strength inside themselves) and this automatically draws out the same in girls.

Choose these people on a simple criteria: that your own soul is drawn to them. They seem at peace, warm-hearted as opposed to merely being 'nice', gutsy and eccentric rather than bland and ordinary. Choose women who are interested in your daughter as an individual, and who see something special in her. It has to be a mutual enjoyment. (At this age the mentor role is safer when it's same-sex, but there may be wonderful exceptions and some women report about having had great male role models too.)

Some activities build soul, while others harm it. Avoid what is intensely competitive or performance-oriented unless your daughter has a real love for these activities and can't be stopped! Creative activity done for its own sake builds your soul; it can be as varied as sculpture, working on motorcycles, or as advanced as writing their own fantasy novel. All these things draw a girl into a sense of peace and reflection, as she is present in doing them.

Books are important as both inspiration and refuge. When we read, we journey inwards – we can't help doing so, as the printed word triggers our own minds to fill in the gaps in a way that a movie can't. And we are taken into other lives, places and times in a way that expands our own sense of what is possible. Many people have had their lives changed by a single book. Adolescents hunger for spirit food, and books often provide this.

Time in nature is something that is often denied to girls because of safety fears. Wandering in woodlands near one's home (the joy of boys since time began) is seen as too risky. But do what you can to provide opportunities for her to be in wild and beautiful places (family holidays are a great way to do this), where she can surf, swim, ride, hike or sail. Do some of these things with her, too, as she needs to see you away from your normal, humdrum self.

SHOULD GIRLS HAVE PRIVACY FROM THEIR MUMS?

A good guide to privacy, which you can explain to your daughter, is if her door is open you can knock and go in. If it's closed, you will knock, then wait for her to say 'come in' before you enter. That's because it's great for her to feel she has some private space and has control over it. When you do go into her room, don't snoop or poke about, nobody likes that. Of course, you can still say 'this room needs tidying', and 'would you like some help?' But just the courtesy of asking her permission gives her a feeling of being respected.

Privacy is a privilege, though, and if she has been doing something secretive or strange (see eating disorders, or having problems with drinking or drugs, pages 192–6 and 201–8) then you may opt to let her know that you will keep an eye out in her room. Safety takes precedence over privacy, but forewarn her all the same. For complicated reasons, it's best if only mum does this. Your daughter can be angry at mum, but she would be outraged if dad were to invade her space. If all is fine, though, privacy is a great thing that we all like to have.

AUNTIES

At the start of this book we pinpointed a huge mental health decline among girls.

We asked how could this be – what is going wrong? One possibility is that we have *forgotten how to do auntie-ing*.

I often ask audiences, 'Who had an auntie who made a big difference in their life?' About a third of all women put their hands up. The older they are, the higher the number. Today, *aunties have progressively disappeared from the lives of girls*.

By Auntie with a capital A, I am referring to real aunties (sisters of her dad or mum); plus adult friends of her mother or your family who take a personal interest in her wellbeing. (Grandmothers have a slightly different role, as an anchor, more than as a role model – their age puts them beyond a girl's imagination!) Every girl needs at least one special Auntie.

As an adult reading this, think of any nieces (or for men, nephews) you may have. Consider if you could be a more-involved Auntie to them? Auntie-ing could mean:

1. Having her over to your house for meals or sometimes to stay. This can be a great respite from home and a chance for real conversations about how they are getting on. If you sense that she is relaxed and likes it, do it every few months. As she begins to feel comfortable with you, when she has crises or deep concerns she is likely to share them with you and seek your advice.
2. Taking her for a regular coffee or shopping trip to town, and talking to her like she is a thoughtful adult. Asking about her life, her dreams, her challenges. Doing it not with a sense of problem-seeking, but of taking the long view, finding out her perspective. Just do a lot of listening.
3. Remembering her birthday, going to her school concerts or sports games.

4. Offering help with practical or financial challenges that she may have in pursuing her dreams. Being sensitive to her mother and father, augmenting just a little the 'team' she has rooting for her.

My auntie paid for my piano lessons.

She took me into the city every school holidays, we had afternoon teas and pretended we were ladies!

When my brother died in a car crash, I went and lived at her house for three months. My parents were just too devastated to function, it was a relief to be somewhere more normal, though I went home at weekends, it was lifesaving for everyone.

My Auntie knew about my boyfriend, and the problems we had, I just couldn't tell Mum.

My Auntie was younger than my mum by about six years, she just understood better. It was her that taught me about menstruation and periods. You could ask her about anything.

I would go to my Auntie's and we would make mosaics together, I just loved doing it with her.

As well as deeply listening, Aunties also talk sense to girls; they know about boys and men and are straight talking.

'Sure, he's good-looking. But he's really dull. You'd be bored after ten minutes.'

'That boy is a player. I wouldn't trust a word he says. He needs ten years to grow up.'

'It's not you he loves, sugar, it's your boobs.'

Aunties also aren't afraid to criticise you. 'You're really just scared of being rejected', 'I think that's wrong – you need to go and tell your mum you're sorry', 'You could do that, but you'd be copping out. You are capable of more than that.'

Auntie-ing and Uncle-ing are much more important than we have realised, but you have to want to do them, or see the need for them and step up. You can't do it on a whim, because young people will be heartbroken if you let them down. It has to be for the long haul – especially through the difficult passage of adolescence. If you feel an affinity with your niece, give it a go. It will be mutually enriching, she will give you a sense of freshness and clarity in return. Aunties are as ancient as the stones, and we are wired to need them.

KEEP CALM AND CARRY ON LOVING ...

Girls get onto an emotional rollercoaster when they hit their teens, and these years can be trying for their parents as they pick their way through the minefield, hoping not to trigger any explosions!

The early teens phase seems to go in two leaps. Firstly, around 13 (sometimes a bit younger), girls seem to become mentally unstuck. The reason is that the rapid rewiring of the prefrontal cortex (which is described on page 31) mostly begins at 13. The effect is that she becomes very babylike, disorganised and helpless. It can be exasperating, but she is just revisiting babyhood. Keep a close watch on her, and enjoy the fact that she at least loves being close, cuddling and hanging out with you. At fourteen, another phase completely kicks in.

Fourteen can be a cranky stage. The teenager has a job to do – to start getting free of her parents. She has been, all being well, embedded in her family and defined by them, and her whole world is part of the family's network. Now that has to change, or she will never make it on her own. It's important not to see this as a rejection process – it isn't based on not liking you. A girl might adore her parents and everything they stand for, but something deep inside her knows that she can't grow from 'inside' her parents' world, she has to get out and be herself. It can lead to all kinds of trying on of identities, such as Goth, punk or grunge appearances to escape a neat and respectable family, to becoming deeply respectable and responsible in a family of hippies! (Remember Saffy in *Absolutely Fabulous?* She's the daughter who is the only remotely decent human being in the entire show!)

Sometimes parents get huffy about this rebellion and back off. But it's not a time for abandoning your daughter. She has to fight, argue, cajole, reason and make a case with someone; it's either you, or the police or her teachers. Better that it's you.

Of course, much of the time she will be just fine, but when she does seem difficult or impossible, don't panic. Deal with it, listen, make your case, grant her some leeway if she argues well, or agree to disagree. She is learning to be her own person, even though she isn't sure what that is yet. It's tough on parents. The old bottom lines about safety and keeping her side of the bargain still count, but get your friendship needs met somewhere else, because your daughter won't want (always) to be your friend at this age.

Fifteen is usually easier, and by 16 most girls have mellowed a great deal. Once she is more sure of herself, she doesn't have to flick you away and she will feel that she can be friends with you again.

EARLY PUBERTY, CHEMICALS AND YOUR GIRL

Many people have been getting alarmed about girls starting puberty sooner, and with good reason. When a girl of eight develops breasts, it's bound to cause her some confusion and bring her undue attention that she could really do without.

Is there an epidemic of early puberty? What's causing it? Is it something in the water? And what can we do to prevent it happening to our daughters?

Puberty is driven by hormones, and for the last hundred years our wonderful industrial system has been making chemicals that mimic those hormones, both on purpose and by accident. Today hormone-mimics and hormone-disruptors like Bisphenol A (BPA) and Pthalates occur in products we use every day and in agricultural chemicals that show up in our water and food.

We've known about this for 40 years.[2] In Italy in 1977, contaminated beef and poultry caused hundreds of boys and girls at a school near Milan to begin growing breasts. Contaminated feed for cattle in Michigan in 1973 affected both milk and beef from those cows, and pregnant mothers who consumed these gave birth to daughters who experienced significantly earlier puberty. And in 2005 a brother and sister aged three and four began growing pubic hair because their dad had been using testosterone cream bought on the internet and normal daily contact with his kids was enough to rub it off on them. Silly man.

Hormones are not like ordinary chemicals – they operate in infinitesimally small doses. A single molecule of hormone is enough to create a reaction, so to talk of 'safe levels' is a scientific nonsense. If hormones are there, they are almost certainly affecting you.

Puberty changes are one effect, but cancer, diabetes, cardiac problems, even behavioural and mental health problems, have also been linked to these chemicals. Harvard School of Public Health, in the US, found that the exposure of *pregnant mums* to BPA correlated with toddlers' behaviour problems, aggressiveness, hyperactivity and raised levels of depression.[3] And importantly, *it was only the girl children that were affected*, indicating that it really was a female hormone being disrupted, probably in their brains while they were in the womb.

The US Department of Health and Human Services looked at hundreds of research studies into the plastics additive BPA and found 'undisputed evidence' that it affects mammary glands. It's fairly safe to say, these chemicals are not good for you, or your girl.[4] So what are we to do?

WHAT CAN YOU DO?

Let's start with the easy ones. Many people have heard that BPA is in polycarbonate water bottles (check for the recycling number 7 on the base) and, until recently, in *baby bottles*. And yes, it does leach out – students in one study who used these bottles had a 69 per cent increase in their levels *after just one week!*[5]

Worse news is that BPA is also found in the liners of cans which are used for vegetables and soups. This is a much greater source than drink bottles because of the longer exposure that food has to the lining, during which it will interact with it. Canned tomato soup, which is slightly acid, is a good one to avoid right away. Canned soft drinks and alcoholic drinks also leach BPA into their contents. If you use baby formula, the powder is a lot safer than liquids. Plastic cling wraps on foods should be avoided, unless you can find one that is BPA-free – and *never* heat them or microwave them.

Finally, BPA is also present on the thermal paper used for supermarket dockets and airline boarding passes, although safe alternatives do exist. For people who work on supermarket checkouts, this is of special concern.

Hormone mimics are also present in agricultural sprays, so eating organic is a good idea if you can, and try to buy grass-fed rather than grain-fed meat. (It's also healthier for you, and of course, the cows.)

Some of the recommendations are really hard to carry out and in fact require legislative change. What the heck can you or I do about furniture treated with fire retardants? How would we know if a mattress or clothing is chemically treated? (If it smells chemical, *it probably is*. Give it a good airing before having it near you. But not all chemicals smell.)

And finally, cosmetics often have pthalates – nail polish and artificial fragrances are common culprits. (Google the Campaign for Safe Cosmetics website for details.) Use fragrance-free detergents, cleansers, personal care products, and avoid air fresheners unless their label clearly states 'pthalate-free'. *Many air fresheners contain phthalates, and of course you breathe these in*.

If this makes you feel like living in a cabin in the woods, I don't blame you. It's the job of politicians and regulators to manage these things, but industry lobbies continually to keep us in the dark. In the meantime, a pregnant mum who works on a checkout, uses nail varnish, drinks soft drink out of a can, heats canned soup for dinner, and eats grain-fed beef should probably hope for a boy!

WHAT TO DO ABOUT PREMATURE PUBERTY

When girls experience premature signs of puberty such as breast growth, there are a range of reasons:

- There are syndromes that cause early puberty, not caused by external hormones, which affect some girls, such as CPP, or central precocious puberty. These girls might show signs of puberty as young as three to six years old, for example. These conditions can be treated by drugs and managed well.
- Completely different to the above, but some girls simply do enter puberty very young and always have done. It is a small proportion, but still a significant number, and it varies hugely by race. By age seven, 10 per cent of white girls, 23 per cent of

black girls, 15 per cent of Hispanic girls and 2 per cent of Asian girls have started developing breasts. Specialists do NOT recommend treating these conditions as they are part of the normal range.

- To say that more girls are entering puberty younger is not strictly true; what is happening is that more and more girls are having breast budding younger, but this is not true puberty – i.e. it does not correspond to the other changes. The age of actual 'menarche' (the start of periods) has changed very little over the last 40 years and is still a little past the age of twelve. (Though it can be as late as 16, so don't worry, there are late 'bloomers' in every group of girls.)

- The researchers into girls who had breast development early found that in many of these girls, the usual oestrogens from the body at puberty (oestradiol) were not present. This lead to the conclusion that it was oestrogen-like chemicals from the environment that were triggering a kind of 'false start'. *Breast growth of this kind did not bring forward the age of first menstruation, and true puberty stayed on its normal track*.

- But this is still a problem. For one thing, early breast growth increases the lifetime risk of cancer and, perhaps more importantly, having breast development at eight or nine brings on social attention which in our sexualised world a girl is far from ready to deal with. It's this latter fact that has caused parents most concern.

There are several other reasons as to why puberty starts sooner, including:

- Having a lot of body fat. Body fat actually creates oestrogen and starts a vicious circle as oestrogen then tells the body to lay down more fat. (See the chapter on weight issues for help with this.) *Don't* let your daughter start dieting or force her into more exercise, as these responses often backfire.

- Having a lot of stress. Girls whose parents divorced between the ages of three and eight, or had fathers who were violent, alcohol- or drug-dependent, suicidal or spent time in prison were more likely to have early puberty.
- Having a stepdad. This is not because stepdads are stressful, but probably because an unrelated male in the home affects girls' hormones in some way we don't understand.
- Being from a developing country or suffering early starvation. Adopted orphans and refugees who have settled in developed countries as young children often show early puberty. Our best explanation for this is that the body decides, life is tough, better get on with it.

So what can you do if your daughter starts puberty really young, say at age seven or eight? We can't change the fact that our daughters start puberty early, but we can change how we deal with it. We can encourage them to be active and enjoy their bodies. We can treat them as the age they are, and not be influenced by the way they look. We can stand up to a world that markets bras (even push-up bras!) for six-year-olds and puts them in beauty pageants with make-up and coy moves. We can keep their childhood happy and relaxed by not buying into competitiveness, by having family meals together, reading books together, and letting them be young. Early puberty can be disconcerting, but it's not a recipe for disaster. We can manage it and keep their lives on track.

IF YOUR DAUGHTER IS SAME-SEX ATTRACTED

There has been enormous progress in the last few years in accepting and understanding young people who are same-sex attracted. There are cabinet ministers, rock stars, athletes, actors, teachers, pastors and broadcasters who are happily and publicly in same-sex relationships and almost nobody blinks an eye.

On the other hand, there are still people who regard lesbian, gay, bisexual or transgender (LGBT)* orientation as some kind of evil choice, or an illness that needs a cure. This viewpoint is, fortunately, decreasing, perhaps as people simply get to know the facts and to know gay people in person.

For a parent, this growing acceptance is helpful, but it still has a fair way to go. Being a parent of a same-sex-attracted daughter is still a road that takes some courage to walk.

The Facts
Society's default assumption is that everyone is straight. Even for the young person concerned, the discovery that he or she is same-sex attracted may come as something of a shock. Then there is the question of how to let others know – especially Mum and Dad. A young person may be terrified that their parents won't accept them, or will react badly to the news. Recognising that you are same-sex attracted usually happens in the early teens, which is a hard-enough time already for fitting in and believing in yourself. This situation needs sensitivity and help from all around your child.

---

* LGBT (Lesbian, Gay, Bisexual, Transgender) is the now commonly accepted term for people who don't fit the neat categories of 'straight' heterosexuality. Gay is sometimes used as shorthand for all categories, but most people use 'lesbian' as the simplest way to denote girls who are primarily attracted to other girls. Transgender girls – who wish to be boys and may or may not actually have treatment to become more male are another category which we haven't addressed in this book. The issues for parents remain the same in terms of acceptance and support for her in discovering who she really is.

Whatever your child's sexual orientation turns out to be, it helps if all through their growing up that *your language* about gay and lesbian people is understanding and not derogatory, and you have taken the trouble to read about or got to know a little of the LGBT experience. A dad (or mum) who mocks or puts down gay people is not going to invite openness in their own kids.

The process of acknowledging, first in oneself, then to one's parents and then one's wider circle of friends and family, is a series of decisions a young person has to think about. Most gay adults will tell you that 'coming out' – letting the world know by degrees that you are not quite what they think you are – is a long journey. *If your daughter discovers she is LGBT, she is the only one who can decide about who she tells, and when. Some young people are totally comfortable, free and proud about their sexual orientation, others not at all so, and this may depend on the attitudes of those around them.*

There is an inner journey for parents too. Long before we become parents, even when we are still children ourselves, we dream of the children we will have. Parenthood is nurtured and powered by thoughts of the future. Our dreams run out ahead of us, and weddings and grandchildren often feature in these fantasies!

The power of these dreams can't be underestimated. Often from their earliest years we get angry with our children for not fitting in to our stereotypes of how they are supposed to be. Letting go of assumptions – all girls will like to cook, or be neat and clean, all boys will want to be noisy and sporting – is very important, or our kids will feel they have somehow failed us.

Learning that your child is lesbian or gay can crash a truck through some of your fondest hopes. We can say we don't care and, out of consideration for our daughters, convince ourselves that we don't mind one bit, but *acceptance isn't just an effort of will*, it's a process you have to go through – and that means grief for what you have lost as well. It's useful to take some time reflecting on this, take a break either alone or together, and just begin to let go of all those half-submerged dreams of 'the daughter you imagined' and the daughter as a real person. Write a journal. Take a few long walks. Allow yourself some time to let go of one reality, and learn to welcome another.

Parents of a lesbian daughter may find that, with her agreement, they want to let their friends know. After all, we all want to be understood and known by our friends. Most will probably be comfortable and welcoming. However, it's possible, depending on the circles you move in, that some friends will be judgemental.

Pamela Du Valle, the mum of a gay son, wrote movingly of this in a poem that includes this verse:

'... I will tell you now and it is up to you
To my son and myself I have to be true
If you do not accept myself and my son
Our friendship is over, over and done.'[6]

This fierce loyalty to one's offspring is a great attribute, and must give enormous heart to her son.

Beyond the transitions of 'coming out', lesbian girls will have the same 'issues' as everyone else: Will I find love? Will I be treated with respect by those around me?

There are whole books on this topic, as well as organisations like Parents and Friends of Lesbians and Gays, that can help you if you have a lesbian daughter. But for any parent, it's worth being well informed. Even if your daughter is straight, she will likely have lesbian friends who will appreciate your being supportive and unfussed.

A final note – lots of girls go through intense friendships in their teens and are very affectionate. These friendships are not usually sexual and are not a sign of sexual orientation one way or the other. (In more open societies, boys too have strong friendships like this as part of growing up.) There is a fashion now for boys at parties etc., to urge girls to 'make out' in imitation of porn movies designed to titillate men. With all this craziness around, girls worry and get tense, and may pull back from friendships needlessly. Encourage your daughter to be herself, and be open with friends, talk about what they feel is and isn't comfortable. There are too many labels put on us all – we are all unique and no label ever describes us.

TEENAGE GIRLS AND SLEEP
BY DR MICHAEL CARR-GREGG

Recently researchers have confirmed what parents always knew – that teenagers don't get enough sleep. Part of the problem is that the sleep cycle shifts in adolescence so that they actually need to sleep in longer. But we inevitably have to wake them to go to school. The accumulated sleep debt is bad for both learning and mental health, but there are remedies ... Australia's foremost adolescent psychologist and mental health campaigner, Dr Michael Carr-Gregg, explains ...

It's 8.30 a.m. and we are standing outside a typical girls' school anywhere in the world. As students emerge from cars and buses, an ocean of sleepy faces appear before us, some grasping take-away lattes in their hands – it's narcolepsy central.

Within half an hour some of these young ladies will have their heads on desks, fast asleep, while others will be so sleep-deprived that they are oblivious to the learning going on around them.

It's official, teenagers – boys and girls – are the most sleep-deprived segment of the population. The world's leading authority in teenage sleep, Professor Mary Carskadon of Brown University, in the USA, found that on average adolescents get about 7.5 hours sleep on school nights, but *25 per cent get 6.5 hours or less*. That's a quarter of all teens ending up seriously sleep deprived. Carskadon found that in order for a young person to be optimally alert, they require *9.25 hours of sleep*. It is increasingly evident to educators and psychologists that night after night many girls are treating sleep as an optional extra, and are building colossal sleep debts.[7]

If you attached an electroencephalograph to those dozing girls, heads down on their desks, we'd see that 50 per cent will go directly into REM sleep; exhibiting the same brain waves as patients with narcolepsy. While these girls don't actually have narcolepsy, nevertheless they're living under conditions that actually make them appear as if they do.

Insufficient sleep not only impacts on girls' physical health, but also dramatically reduces their capacity to perform and respond appropriately while sitting in a classroom, driving a car, playing sport or interacting with adults. It increases rates of depression, and even increases suicidal feelings and thoughts. From an academic point of view, a good night's sleep is the most powerful study aid there is.

Schools must start teaching 'bed-ucation' because adolescents need to know how a lack of sleep impacts on the 100 billion brain cells and one trillion connections. Parents need to make sleep a priority, and set limits and boundaries around bedtime from an early age. Finally, perhaps we need to start reviewing the issue of school starting time. Studies have found that a starting time for secondary school of even half an hour later creates a marked gain in health and wellbeing, as well as learning.

What to Do?

Have an evening routine and clear bedtimes. Reading in bed to chill out for half an hour is fine, but do not allow electronic media – phones, iPads, computers or TVs – in bedrooms (screens affect the brain's readiness for sleep, apart from the content being too stimulating).

Teens may need to sleep in at weekends to clear their sleep-debt. This is a healthy catch-up, but it's better if they get nine hours a night during the week.

Because of the time shift in adolescence, schools should not start too early. We need to change school schedules to suit teenagers' bodies better.

Chapter 6

Preparing for Adulthood

(14–18 years)

Imagine a girl of 14. She's halfway through secondary school. She's almost grown to her full height, and she's come through puberty. She is capable of having a baby. She is strong, coordinated, and quite smart. (A few hundred years ago – or in Afghanistan – she would be getting married now.) So, what do you think? Is she ready for womanhood?

The answer will be clear to anyone with a 14-year-old daughter. Probably not! The qualities that make up maturity are emerging at fourteen, *but like a dodgy light globe, they flicker on and off*. One minute she can be kind and caring, but another minute she can be thoughtless and self-obsessed. She can make great promises but forgets to keep them. She can lose all perspective. She's very prone to peer pressure. She can be wildly overemotional.

None of this is her fault – an early-teenage girl's brain is still setting up its centre of control in the prefrontal cortex, and it's like a 'head office' that isn't finished yet. She can go there, but not for long. The part of her brain called the amygdala – the centre of impulsive and emotional reactions – may take over in a flash if she is pressured, distracted or stressed.

It's true that in a traditional society a girl often got married at fourteen, but in those societies, cast-iron rules about acceptable behaviour shackled her and defined every second of her life. Today we seek a very different womanhood for our daughters – independent, not proscribed by gender roles, and equal in opportunity to any man. *Achieving that kind of womanhood takes a little longer.*

The years from 14 to 18 are a time of intense preparation because modern womanhood is tough. Your daughter will need to be self-reliant, clear thinking, emotionally strong, good with people and responsible for her own life. Even better still, she will have a sense of purpose and be attuned to what makes life meaningful and good. These are your final blessings to her, before you send her out into the future.

What Makes You an Adult?

Today we consider adulthood begins somewhere between the ages of 18 and 21. So by 18 a girl needs to be 'there' in terms of being able to function independently and well. She can legally drive a car, work, have sex, drink alcohol, and make her own choices in every way, so we have to make sure she can do so without damaging or killing herself or anyone else. But it's more than just staying out of trouble, a real adult has her own goals and purpose in life, she has figured out what is really important. So between 14 and 18, this is what we aim for with our girls.

In this chapter we'll tell you the stories of two young women who make the journey from girlhood to womanhood. One is the survivor of a serious accident, the other is a famous singer who almost lost her career, until she was able to work out why she was in the world. For all girls, hopefully in less dramatic ways, the same lessons have to be learned. 'Your life is in your hands. Other people's lives are in your hands. Welcome to the terrifying freedom of adulthood!'

PARENTS WHO COP OUT

Some parents DO let their daughters grow up at 14. This seems to be the result of a dual wish: to have their daughters as friends (so much easier than actually raising them), and to feel young themselves, to be hip and cool instead of strong and caring (which is hard work). These are the parents who buy the booze for the party, the dads who slip their daughter £50 for going out on the town. So you get daughters acting too old, and parents acting too young. They joke about her being '14 going on 20' when they themselves are 45 going on 15. It's a betrayal, because daughters don't need friends, they desperately need parents who step up to being in charge by setting curfews, driving to pick them up at an agreed time, saying no to alcohol when they are underage, and knowing where they are and who they are with. They need parents who are willing to be a little unpopular to save their daughter's life.

Initiation Into Womanhood

Old societies knew a lot about raising the young. They did things that only now our best neuroscience is proving right. For example, they deeply loved and indulged their babies and young children, delighting in them and letting them play and be unfettered. They expected much more of their six- to 12-year-olds, giving them jobs and responsibilities, and they always, without exception, put a lot of energy into their mid-adolescents, kickstarting them, exploding them almost, into adulthood. *Becoming an adult was never left to chance.*

There has been a lot of interest in recent years in the idea of parents and other caring adults creating adolescent 'rites of passage'. A rite of passage is a time of intensified activity, teaching, ritual and involvement that says to a girl, 'we will help you and celebrate you in becoming a woman'.

In Australian schools, programmes like the Rite Journey, and Pathways to Womanhood are becoming widespread. These programmes take the girls out of their usual world, to a place where they can spend time over several days with older women including their mothers, female mentors and teachers. The girls listen to stories about womanhood from these women, and are invited to make declarations of their own identity and values. The adults praise and affirm the girls' positive qualities, what they see in them, and invite them to say goodbye (and thank you) to girlhood.

Suffused through this is a sense of pride and honour in being a woman, a sense that has often disappeared from girls' views of themselves, with tragic consequences. At the end of these programmes, the girls re-enter the normal world, and as part of this their fathers greet them in a ceremony that acknowledges they are now women, not girls.

Whether we participate in a formal programme or simply take on the challenge ourselves as the parents and family of a girl, the same elements have to be there.

The question that we have to challenge our daughters with at this age boil down to this: 'what kind of woman do you want to be?' A girl may answer in many different ways ...

'I am true and trustworthy with my friends.'

'I am in this world to help others.'

'I am a leader, and want to take people to a better world.'

'I am a creator, and want to make beauty.'

'I am proud of being different and unique.'

The dangers of being a woman need to be honestly discussed and put in perspective. Childhood is protected; womanhood is not. As one girl put it to me: 'It's no longer my parents mucking up my life. I am free now to muck up my own life!'

A girl who has had a 'rite of passage' isn't fully a woman yet, she is a *beginning woman*. But she has crossed the river, her sights are set on the future, and she is not going back.[1]

Even Chores Teach You to Be Adult

Rites of passage are just the tip of the iceberg of growing up. Underneath lies all the work that mothers and fathers do to teach the joys of 'mucking in' – being a helpful and eventually equal contributor around the house and in the community. Parents have to make this happen for one important reason: *nobody would grow up if they didn't have to.*

It's not done out of meanness or just a wish to get help with cooking, running errands or paying the bills! These certainly matter, but it's what they represent, and teach. Doing things for others creates an inner shift. We make the dinner, or make our room a clean, neat and functional place. We earn money at the weekends to pay for some of our bills, *and on the inside we feel proud, capable and free.*

Expect a lot of repetitive and careful teaching to take place around daily living. Do this with optimism and empathy, rather than nagging or whining. Be patient and empathic (but insistent). You are her coach, and you have to be 'welcome inside her head' for your message to really embed: 'I know you're tired, but let's get started and we can soon have it done, then we can all take it easy.'

You can help your daughter (or son) hugely by simply making sure they always:

- *Put away, wash, or tidy up what they have used.*
- *Keep their stuff in order so they can find things easily when needed.*
- *Have good manners and speak respectfully to people, whether strangers or family.*
- *Treat other people's property with respect.*
- *Apologise when they have done the wrong thing, make amends and fix the problem they have caused.*

Teenagers who don't pull their weight and let others clean up after them create a negative energy which saps everyone's happiness, including their own. The knack is to develop the habit of doing it right so that it's automatic and there is no energy expended or doubt needed. You can get on with having a great time because the environment is efficient, clean and easy to be in. It's so much easier to start this way and just keep it happening.

Of course, this is just the day-to-day stuff, also waiting out there is the big world.

That takes it all to a whole new level ...

Responsibility –
The Toughest Lesson There Is

Marielle, aged 14, was a happy and athletic girl. She was the oldest of four children and attended a co-ed secondary school in the western suburbs of Sydney, Australia. One spring afternoon, she and her friends poured laughing and chatting through the school gates and out towards the train station to travel home. They crossed at a set of pedestrian lights just outside the school, in a large group, just as they had every single day. But this time, they barely had time to turn their heads as the screech of brakes came micro-seconds before a large car ploughed into them.

One girl was killed instantly, another five, including Marielle, were seriously injured.

Marielle was in hospital for almost six months. Multiple operations reconstructed her body, painful and intense rehabilitation had her able to walk, and while she will never be quite as able-bodied again, she can live a normal life. Except for one thing: she is terrified of going anywhere near a road. She has agoraphobia and suffers nightmares and flash-backs. She can be driven to school, but it's an ordeal for her and her parents.

Her parents sought out counselling for her, with a woman counsellor in her 50s who specialises in trauma, and over several months Marielle was taught relaxation and mindfulness skills, worked through what happened and built up her mental strength. She improved considerably, but she is still not able to go near a road that has cars on it. If she tries, she begins to tremble uncontrollably, feels nauseated, and suffers attacks of diarrhoea. These are the same symptoms that combat soldiers often suffer when they return home from war or a dangerous tour of duty, it is a condition whose name everyone knows now: Post Traumatic Stress Disorder.

Marielle's counsellor is a very capable and creative woman who has become like a kind of feisty aunt to Marielle, able to soothe her but also to push her when needed. She is ready with the next step. They have been meeting for over three months. (I would not advise the following strategy ever be used unless a relationship is strong and well established.)

Marielle, we've talked about what happened on that day, you've gradually pieced it together.

Yes.

There's something else we haven't talked about.

Mmm?

When you talk about or think about the accident that happened that day, who do you blame?

The driver, the stupid idiot that killed my friend, that smashed me up.

(Marielle's words are angry, but her look is sad, she is tearing up now, as she often does when she talks about it.)

Okay, so you think the driver was 100 per cent to blame?

Yes.

And you were an innocent victim of that?

Yes, and unlucky too.

The counsellor pauses, draws a deep breath.

Do you feel you have any share in the blame?

There is a kind of 'booming silence', this question is a jolting one, and though she does not show it, Marielle's mind reels.

What do you mean?

You crossed on a green light ...

Yes. We always look, it'd be stupid not to.

Was there anything else you could have done?

There is a pause.

How do you mean?

The counsellor is silent. The pair know each other well now, this turn of conversation could not have been taken without very considerable rapport.

Marielle finally speaks ...

I still don't know what you mean?

Did you look to see if there was a car coming?

We didn't need to, it was a green light for us to walk.

So you didn't look?

Marielle just stares back at the counsellor, their eyes lock, but inside her brain, wheels are spinning.

In the weeks that follow, Marielle plunges into another layer of dealing with what life has dealt her. The victim position was so easy to take;

she was a child, innocently crossing at a green light, with dozens of schoolmates with her. They could not have expected a car to speed into them, but they did not check – and one did.

Who could allocate the responsibility in this? The driver was 100 per cent responsible, and was in jail as a result, but Marielle suddenly grasped that she had been too trusting, too unaware of her environment, too distracted to really check she was safe. Cars don't always stop at red lights. Not all drivers are sane or sober. She should have looked.

Of course part of Marielle knew this, as did everyone around the situation, but no one said so. Who would have had the heart to add blame to the suffering she had already gone through? But this counsellor knew that the truth mattered, and that Marielle knew that too.

Momentarily, Marielle plunged into the opposite extreme, from 'no blame' to 'all the blame'. She agonised that she could have saved her friend's life if she had just been more alert. But the counsellor was ready for this, and they continued to evaluate, drawing now on the strong bond of trust to do some tough talking.

'You trusted the drivers to do the right thing, because they always did. The lights were green. That had always worked in the past. But you can't trust all drivers. You should have looked. SO SHOULD EVERY OTHER GIRL ON THAT CROSSING. It might not have saved them. But it might.'

Gradually, Marielle took on her own sliver of responsibility, no more, no less.

In a deeper sense, this was a lesson called 'growing up'. It was timely; at 14 a girl really is entering womanhood, and part of being an adult is knowing that the world is random and cruel, and you have to watch your back. You can hugely improve your safety by being wide awake and savvy.

In the weeks that followed, the lesson became not just a thought but a part of Marielle's body too. The horrible injuries she had sustained had been contributed to, in just a small part, by her own behaviour. She could change that behaviour. She could be less a victim and more the agent of her own fate. Taking even 5 per cent of the blame was a painful lesson, but an empowering one too. Cars ARE dangerous, but much more so if you don't watch out for them. Somehow, along with this realisation, Marielle's fear went away. She began to approach roads, not with her head down and trembling, but with a fierce eye on what was going on.

Marielle now goes over that crossing, and much more besides, with just a flicker, just a brief moment, of quiet determination, staring down death, knowing that death is always right alongside us. She is glad to be alive, determined to stay that way. She is not just healed, she is grown-up.

The Real Secret of Adulthood

Now it's time for a very advanced idea. This is deep water, but I hope you will go there with me. I have come to believe that the biggest difference between an adult and a child is *knowing why you are in the world*.

Consider this for a moment: a child is in the world for him- or herself. That's appropriate and right, but it's not our ultimate goal. The highest happiness, according to both ancient wisdom and the most modern research in positive psychology, comes when we step outside our own importance and learn how to care for the big picture – the big life, not just our own small life.

This can easily be mistaken (especially given the history of women's lives) for being a martyr and living only for others. That's not what I am saying here.

There is a place where our own deepest needs – what we really love to do – intersect with the needs of the world we live in. When we find that place, it's all pure joy.

The following story will help you to understand what I mean.

A Singer Finds Her Soul[2]

Missy Higgins is an Australian musician and singer who is acclaimed worldwide for the raw beauty and authenticity of her songs. This talented woman started young; she signed a worldwide record deal when she was still in Year 12 at school. The songs on her first album had been hammered out on the practice piano in the school's music room. Then, suddenly, she was on a world stage. But the meteoric fame and exposure left her staggering, overwhelmed by panic attacks, and physically incapable of going on stage.

There had been warning signs earlier, including a hospitalization in Year 11 after a nervous collapse. It was then that she learned that her father had also suffered from depression throughout his life, which he had managed to overcome.

Missy withdrew from performing completely, instructing her agent to send no offers, no invitations or even to email, which he abided by for almost two years. She spent time in ashrams, travelled widely, saw a therapist, went to university and worked hard to heal her life from the implosive forces of too much success too soon on a vulnerable and open heart.

It wasn't an easy time – a soul journey is never easy – but then something happened. Perhaps it was chance, or perhaps it was the natural result of all those sincere attempts to journey towards the truth. Acting on instinct, her agent broke his silence and sent her an invitation to perform at an all-women festival called Lilith Fair, in the United States. Something inside her said 'yes, do this' ...

Her performance was awesome. Afterwards, grateful fans surrounded her, thanking her warmheartedly for what her music had given them over the years. She suddenly realised that *the musical gift she had was for other people*. That she had something to offer to the human race.

She has gone back to writing, recording and performing her songs. I suspect this is something that all true, enduring performers have to realise: that 'it's not about me'. The anxiety and pressure to succeed, the sense of exposure and vulnerability, somehow dissolve when you real-

ise you stand in grace, and that you are there to give love to your listeners.

The meaning of art is to lift up your fellow human beings to a higher place. It's precious and special and you have to honour it. Self is lost in the joining. This is what we mean by soul.

By 18, or 20, or 25, whenever it comes, a girl arrives at somewhere awesome: the beginning of womanhood. She knows that she holds the reins of her own life. She knows that the key to happiness is not in self-seeking. She feels connected to life and that she has a part to play in the human race. The real adventure can begin.

Dreaming Forward

This chapter ends the five stages of growing a girl into a woman. As a way to finish up, let's do some dreaming. Whatever age your girl is now, it's great to glimpse and even begin to aim for the woman she will become. So settle back in your chair or pillow, and come on a journey ...

You are in a peaceful house, on a leafy street. It's evening, and still warm after a sunny summer's day. You are older, but still strong and well. You glance out of your window and see out on the road that a car is pulling up. It's an electric car, silent, compact and sleek.

Stepping out of the car is a young woman, as you look closer you realise it's your grown-up daughter. How does she look? What kind of clothes is she wearing?

Does she have a partner with her? Children? You go out to greet her. Can you see what kind of person she is, what qualities shine from her? How has she changed? What is her voice like? How tall is she? Is she fit and well? What kind of things has she been doing with her time and talents? Let your imagination fill in the details.

Bring her inside your house, sit down and talk. What is she telling you? How are you feeling? See the connections between the childhood you gave her and the strengths and qualities she now has. Feel proud and deeply satisfied. A fine woman will live on after you are gone, and she will pass on what you have taught and given her down the generations.

In a Nutshell

- Preparing a girl for womanhood requires a lot of teaching in the years from 14 to 18.
- Rites of passage are needed to make the leap. It doesn't happen without help.
- Work and responsibility are a necessary part of training to be an adult.
- Marielle learned from a terrible accident that she holds the reins of her own life.
- A talented singer found peace in giving. Adulthood means escaping from the prison of self and being part of the big life.
- You can't form good relationships until you are strong in your own right.
- The age of 18 is not womanhood, but it is the start of womanhood.

Part Two

Hazards and Helps

The Six Big Risk Areas and How to Navigate Them

Chapter 7

The Rush We're All In

Two Girlhoods, Two Ways of Life

Carrie sleeps long and deep – the only sounds all night are the wind in the trees and the rain on her bedroom roof. When she wakes and parts the curtain, she can see the sun through the branches. She wanders downstairs. Her parents are talking amiably in the kitchen but stop to greet her and she slides into a sideways hug beside her mum, not wanting to interrupt their conversation. They don't seem to mind – in fact her dad asks if she wants a pancake. She asks if he can save her one and wanders outside to call her dog for a walk up the hill behind their house. She loves this time of day, the chance to think and dream and wake up slowly. She is looking forward to getting back to her artwork project in the shed – it's taken weeks now and is near to completion. She loves the springtime. Her legs feel strong as she strides over the uneven ground, the dog jumping back and forth to urge her on.

Karla wakes at six to her phone alarm. Her mother calls out to her from down the hall not to dawdle – they have to leave in half an hour because of the roadworks. It's a long commute to her school. Her mum will take her today and she'll go to the before-school care room – she can catch up on homework there, she hopes. It's only three weeks until the exams. She skips breakfast – she feels a bit ill and it's a good chance to lose a few calories. 'Shit!' She's still got to put on her make-up. Her mother is yelling at her to do it in the car. Her dad has to leave soon too – Karla's little brother needs driving to his school which is in the oppo-site direction. Her brother pulls a face at her across the table, and mouths the word 'fat' silently at her. She hates him so much. Six years old and already an arsehole. Typical boy. Her phone pings. It's a friend – something has gone wrong with another friend. She spends the forty minutes in the car messaging. Her mother knows better than to ask what is going on. 'You wouldn't understand, Mum, it's not like when you were a girl.'

Both these girls are fifteen. They live about 50 kilometres apart. Their lives couldn't be more different.

In a special section at the end of this book, we'll describe the '10 Things Girls Need Most', a list based on thousands of studies of girl-hood around the world over the last 40 years. Two of those things are exposure to nature and having a rhythmic, peaceful life with time to breathe in, dream, integrate one's life events, and rebond to loved ones and get support from them.

All children, even teenagers, need these two things. Adolescence is such a time of rapid internal (brain and body) development that we actually need to slow life down to help them the best. For example, large amounts of sleep are needed to protect a teenager's changing brain. Rather than more input and stimulation, kids at this age some-times need less going on and more time to dream. They sometimes need more adult care now than when they were in late primary school, yet so often we parents back away. For teens, it has to be relaxed, responsive care which doesn't intrude, create pressure and manipu-late. An important part of the 'work' of adolescence is taking more control of your life, and if they feel you trying to shape them, then this attacks their growing need to be their own person and they naturally and healthily rebel. All the same, teenagers still need to be loved, not merely managed.

It's astonishing how many teens are emotionally abandoned, even within outwardly normal families. At a very expensive school I worked in this year, teachers told me of kids who are there (in organised 'care' which the school provides) from 7.30 a.m. until 9.00 p.m., when they are finally picked up by a parent to go home. A similar school nearby offers boarding for kids whose families only live ten minutes from the school – but whose 'lifestyle' means they can't 'be there' for their kids on weeknights. And in many homes – rich, poor, and in-between, there are many teens who barely speak to their parents or vice versa. Or have any idea of each other's lives.

But even caring parents who get quite obsessed about parenting and worry more and more about their children have somehow strayed far from the conditions their children really need. All over the world mental health experts are pointing out this paradox – that in pursuing some future happiness, one day, we make our kids' lives miserable in the now. Kids perceive this pressure very clearly – 'you must work hard, do well, keep it up, try your hardest, don't ever slacken off and then, one day, you will be a success'. But what might the cost be of this success? Able to afford a coke habit and a divorce lawyer and a therapist? I think this craziness has just crept up on us. We human beings are such herd animals that often our only reality check is 'it's what everyone else is doing, so it must be right'. But what if the herd is going the wrong way?

Every school I work in, all over the world, reports a bad situation with girls. Huge numbers of girls are self-harming, vomiting their meals secretly after dinner, driving themselves with diets or exercise or studying so hard that they become like a tightly wound string of stress. And then, inevitably, they snap.

Perhaps you have had this happen. You wake up in the night to a sound, a human sound that you can't figure out, and stumble down the hall to find your daughter of 14 or 15 sobbing and shuddering on the cold bathroom floor. She has come out of her room, seeking help but not wanting to be a bother, and ended up halfway. That's the last sleep you will get that night. In the morning come the phone calls to doctors for urgent appointments, the psychiatrists' waiting lists, the counselling sessions if you are rich or lucky enough to find someone good. Perhaps time in hospital. Siblings on the back burner. A whole family on edge about whether she might do something to hurt herself. Months and years of building back to a normal life again, something approaching peace of mind and a day without crippling anxiety.

What would you do to avoid this? Prevention is certainly the best way. I know of many families who just decided from some instinct or misgiving about where life was heading to get off the conveyor belt – to take a year out and drive around Australia or Europe, camping. Or to up stakes and move to the country and a quieter life for everyone. Or for one or both parents to have six months or a year off work to be there for the kids. And so on. Anything you do will help. It needn't be so huge, it might be just tweaking – many families bring in a rule of just one out-of-school activity per child. No more rushing about every night of the week to classes and trainings and self-improvement. Saturdays at home in pyjamas, watching dumb videos together as a family or mother-daughter ritual. Fish and chips at the beach on Sunday. Circuit breakers, time to get back into a good rhythm.

These thoughts might strike a chord with you, touch on something you have been thinking yourself, or connect with a yearning in your heart. Perhaps your marriage needs this too. Again, be tough-minded – what would a divorce do to your kids? What would slowing down and making changes do to save your family? There might be friction at first as you discover how far you have drifted apart, how much misunderstanding has built up. It's like taking out the rubbish – it can accumulate for years! But the love underlying your life that has dwindled as you battled the world outside and neglected the world inside will return with some peace and time. Our girls – many of them – are the sensitive ones in the family, and often the first to crack. (Boys go the other way, bottling it up and later in their teens using alcohol or drugs or smashing up cars to lower their pain and anxiety.) Girls are the canaries in the mine.

HOW TO STRENGTHEN SELF-BELIEF

Many families, while they are together, are not really together. It's all rush and hurry, followed by retreat into rooms and screens. Educator Kim McCabe, whose work is mentioned elsewhere in this book, suggests a simple measure in her book *From Daughter to Woman*.[1] Here it is in her own words.

Girls' Together Time

The idea of Girls' Together Time is that mother and daughter – just one daughter at a time if you have a few – have a regular monthly date when they do something together. They set aside a few hours to have fun, really talk or share a simple pleasure or to do something they've both been longing to do. The point is that it's together, and regular, and time she can count on. It can be as creative, simple, adventurous, ordinary, inexpensive, extravagant or experimental as you wish. It could just be going out for a meal. It could be different every time, with choosing what to do being half the fun. Start doing this in her late primary school years, perhaps by age eight or nine. (Earlier, you are already often together. It's in the late primary years that your relationship can start to become weakened if you don't nurture it deliberately.) Once your daughter realises that you plan to take this time together every month, she feels your commitment to her. Children feel loved and special when you give them your time. (And if you think that you cannot find a few hours once a month to spend in this way with your daughter, then perhaps this indicates an imbalance in your lives …)

Girls' Together Time with your daughter can form the basis of a healthy on-going relationship with her into the teenage years. Puberty is a time of such rapid change, a magical time, but a time when your daughter needs you close. You can prepare her. One day your daughter will begin to bleed once a month. This monthly treat of Girls' Together Time should then shift to the week of her menstruation and can become a valuable pressure-release-valve where you can give her the opportunity to talk, sound off, weep, take a break and feel your support.

Girls' Together Time is a simple idea and its power is not immediately obvious. However, many mothers report amazing developments in their relationships with their daughters as a direct result. Try it!

P.S. In aiming to stay close to your daughter, don't be possessive. Other women are important to her development too. Do notice when your daughter warms to another woman and encourage the special connection. Inviting other women to take a mentoring or auntie role with your daughter will enrich both their lives.

So, there are two girlhoods. It shows up in every statistic or study that is published about girls. On the surface, things look okay. But dig down into the findings ('disaggregate – is the technical term) and you find a subgroup headed in the other direction. It's there with teenage drinking. Overall, young people are drinking less (and young men least of all). But a subgroup of girls, about one in eight, are drinking terrifying amounts, bingeing most weekends, sometimes ending up passed out or in emergency rooms, or having blackouts and waking up with no idea where they were or what they did.[2] It's the same with sex. Overall, teenagers are waiting longer than our generation did, taking better birth control precautions, and being more careful about starting into sexual relationships. But one in eight girls are starting younger (often around 14, but sometimes as young as 12) and they are having more partners, more short-term relationships or merely one night stands.[3] When you are this age, sustaining a relationship – or even caring if it is sustained – is beyond the skills or maturity of almost any kid. So, you end up having lots of what now has a name – hook-ups.

When adults are not close and supportive, kids look for affirmation elsewhere. They are being wildly unguided on the internet, hanging out with dangerous adults, being trolled or sending nude images that get misused. Or they go in to overdrive – obsessed with perfection in body or mind, taking their cue from our parental ambitions, the values of their high-achieving school or teachers or the body shaming culture of Instagram, they diet to within an inch of their lives.

Friends of mine in Ireland heard sounds early one morning and found their 15-year-old-daughter in the kitchen throwing up in the sink – she had gone out in the dark to run the streets to lose weight after being bullied at school for being fat. The bullying wasn't just verbal – kids had been slapping her and knocking her to the ground in the playground. She didn't tell anyone, just set out to be thin.

It's our job, whether as a dad, mum, grandparent, school principal, auntie or uncle, next-door neighbour or friend, to step in and befriend, reassure, value and cherish these girls. They look tough, hard and self-reliant, and it suits us to talk about 'resilience' as if it's a character choice (it partly is, but not really until we are about 40 years old!). But they are fragile, vulnerable and designed to be in supporting, friendly, intimate surroundings which our world does not provide.

The Girls Journeying Together puberty-support groups, the wonderful innovation pioneered by Kim McCabe and described on pages

89–91, are simply putting back what was the birthright of girls for millennia – caring adult fi gures specifi cally to hold them through the transition years to womanhood. Th e internet and the shopping mall are not going to do that. But we can, and we can do it for each other's daughters.

There are two girlhoods. There are worlds apart, though they exist in the very same street. One is nurturing and slow, woven with caring adults. One is like a lonely windswept place, with the night coming on and hyenas circling.

Be sure that your girl has the girlhood that she deserves and so desperately needs. Providing that is the job of us adults. We have to make the choices, put in the time, fence out the pressures – she can't do that on her own. Which kind of girlhood will your daughter have – happy and free, or caged in by the world's random demands, judgements, and expectations? You get to choose.

In a Nutshell

- Within a few miles' distance, girls can be living lives of horrendous pressure or natural and rhythmic peace.
- We have to make decisions about our family life so that it supports mental health.
- The absolute heart of this is winning back time so that we can stay close, breathe in, and be restful so that our daughters' brains develop well and their mental health becomes strong.
- Mother and daughter time on a special regular basis helps make you close and able to tackle anything that is going awry in her life.
- Stress reduction through slowing life down is the key to your daughter growing up well.

Chapter 8

Too Sexy Too Soon

During the four years I was working on this book, I talked to anyone who would listen about what they thought was happening to girls. Hairdressers, cab drivers and people seated beside me on planes were soon plunging into the topic. Friends, family and colleagues, everyone said the same thing: *girls are growing up too fast.*

The signs are familiar to every parent. Most eight-year-old girls are already worried about their figure. There are 12-year-olds who won't go outside without putting on make-up. Magazines aimed at 10- to 14-year-olds discuss oral sex. We seem to have just let this happen, without asking if it's a good idea. But clearly it's not.

I have a friend, a feisty and tireless young woman, who is a campaigner for the mental health of girls. She visits schools and talks to the girls about the pressures in their lives. One day she received this letter ...

You don't know me. I was just one of those girls in the audience today. But it was like you were speaking just to me.

Until today I thought that, because I have small breasts, I would have to get breast implants to be a real woman. Also, until today I believed what my friends said – that if I hadn't had sex by the time I was 16, I was a loser.

After hearing you, and all you had to say, I don't think those things any more. I feel so happy and strong. You told me that I am all right, just as I am. Until I heard you, I never believed that.

I am crying as I write this. I can't thank you enough for your message, and for giving it to all girls like me.

This letter is at the same time inspiring, sad, and infuriating. Our daughters should, after 40 years of feminism, feel free to choose, to be themselves, they should know deep in their bones that they are valuable and unique. Yet girls have never been more insecure. How they look, and their 'hotness', has become a constant obsession. Some girls think of little else.

Being evaluated in terms of how pleasing you are to others, how you rate as a 'product' has taken girls back 50 years. Sexualization – the forcing of a sexual identity onto someone from the outside, was a term originally applied in cases of child sexual abuse. Today it's a problem seen in every primary school. It isn't new, but it's much stronger, and more pervasive. Few girls escape it.

#MeToo in School

Some years ago a friend of mine, one of Australia's best-known political journalists, went for a job interview with the country's biggest magazine mogul. Back then she was young and this was an exciting career break. He was a man who politicians feared and who controlled thousands of employees. He told her, with a lip-licking smile, that sex was required to get the job, though he didn't put it so politely. His exact words were 'It's yours. But it'll cost you a fuck'. It sounded like he meant *right now*. She ran from his office, shaking uncontrollably, and never went back. It was the most sickening moment of her life.

It's been a dark, infuriating fact of life for women and girls for centuries. If you worked around men with power – from a factory supervisor or cafe owner right through to a corporate CEO – and especially if you were young, you were a target. Being pressured for sexual favours, harassed, humiliated or even sexually assaulted was a hazard of the workplace. Not every workplace, but more than you would guess. If you were lucky, the other girls or women warned you who to watch and where not to go. Every parent sending their daughter to her first part-time job or job interview felt this in the pit of their stomach. Will she be safe? What an outrageous thing to have to worry about.

The #MeToo movement of the last couple of years was the point where people said – enough. Women speaking up has meant that some horrible men have been stopped in their tracks. A start has been made.

But now we are realising something even more horrible. It starts young. In secondary school for sure, and even in primary school. Last year on Sydney's northern beaches, two 12-year-old boys raped a six-year-old girl in the toilets of her suburban primary school. We can barely imagine how horrific this was for this little girl, or what the effects on her mental health or future wellbeing would be. Or the anguish of her parents and family, having assumed that school was a safe place for her to be. Despite the boys being charged by police, a judge ruled that at the age of 12 they did not understand that what they did was morally wrong and dismissed the case. Which is rather hard to fathom (in the UK the age of culpability in such a crime is 10). Perhaps Australian boys are slow learners.[1]

The problem is everywhere. In the UK in 2015 it was reported that 5500 sexual assaults had occurred in schools in the preceding three years, including hundreds of actual rapes.[2] The effects on these girls (and boys) is profoundly traumatic. One mum described her daughter as having become 'an empty shell'. Today, psychologists know that when self-harm is discovered in a child, finding out if they have been sexually abused is the first thing to investigate. It's that common.[3]

The school system has been dismally slow in catching up. It's clear that perpetrators should be moved away from victims (and not the reverse), so that they can feel safe, understand that their trauma is taken seriously and be reassured that what has happened is not their fault. It's also clear that treatment must be made mandatory for the boys responsible. But prevention is clearly better still. Lessons on consent and sexual boundaries need to be taught at a much younger age so there is no chance of saying 'we didn't know it was wrong'; and so that victims have the language to be able to speak up.

Rape or assault are at the end of an abuse continuum that almost every girl in school experiences today. My colleague Melinda Tankard Reist is a former journalist who now specialises in ending the sexual mistreatment of girls. Almost every week Melinda can be found standing in front of large school assemblies, talking about this problem.

Then she meets with the kids in small group discussions. Here is what the girls in one private Catholic school in suburban Sydney reported as their experience.

- *Having your bum grabbed or breasts touched as you go through crowded corridors every single day.*
- *Being asked for 'head' by boys during the recess or lunch break.*
- *Having boys grab their own genital area in front of you or rubbing their crotch against you while passing you in the classroom or corridor*
- *Being called a snitch, frigid, or a dog if you speak up or complain about any of these things.*
- *Being told by a boy that 'you are a group project,' meaning a gang of boys which he belonged to were planning to get you alone.*
- *A girl known to be a rape survivor having rape jokes and taunts made to upset her.*
- *Messages on social media when you get home that 'your arse looked so good today.' Or negative or insulting comments about sexual features or threats to rape you.*

- *Being asked out, or even have a boy make friends with you,
  only to find out it was on a dare and for the amusement of their
  mates if they managed to 'score' with you.*

These boys have developed or learned a culture where girls are not people but targets, prey for humiliation, for sexual excitement, for scoring points with each other, and for egging each other on to grosser acts. This 'rape culture' says it's okay and natural and normal to behave this way. Then it's no surprise when, individually or in groups, kids carry out actual assaults. This is the very opposite of what manhood should mean. It's creep behaviour and we need both men and women in schools teaching boys that it's wrong and won't turn out well.

The effect on girls – a whole generation of girls – is that they simply feel beleaguered. They think it's normal, and there is something wrong with them when they don't like it or don't feel okay about it. Being constantly evaluated and compared, menaced or objectified, never able to relax or just be themselves. Not remotely safe.

What Can Be Done

One of the girls summed it up: 'We have given up, stopped trying. It is embarrassing this is what we have to put up with after all the talk about equality. We shouldn't have to worry about this.' Melinda's reply: 'No girls, you really shouldn't. We promise to do all we can so that one day you won't have to.'

What can we do as parents? We have to talk to our daughters and say 'we know about this and it isn't right'. Schools must address it formally (and not with sanctimonious lectures at assembly, but in close-up small group discussions, and education inputs that get very specific and ask about the girls' experiences). There needs to be detailed and intense work with boys about how to have equal and positive relationships with girls, because this stuff won't work for them either in their own lives. Schools need clear procedures to ensure that reports of this kind of behaviour are always treated seriously[4]. Romantic and sexual attraction is always part of young people being together, but this has shifted to a much uglier and more dehumanised place. Young love, once one of the most special things about being a teenager, is now often frightening and disillusioning, one more hazard to be endured in being a girl. We have to fix this.

NUDE SELFIES, AND OTHER STUFF WE NEVER HAD TO CONTEND WITH

Following her screen presentation on the pressures that come from advertising, magazines, and the internet, Melinda often chats with kids to ask what they took from the session. Here three girls – all of them aged 14, at a private co-ed school in Sydney – talk about sending nude photos to boys. It's part horrifying, and part encouraging. These are gutsy girls, just waking up to things, with good humour but some serious annoyance too.

Sarah: Well, you really changed our perspective on, like, how we view like – what guys do to us, and that we shouldn't feel pressured, to – like – look a certain way to please them!

Peta: Yeah, I've been asked to send naked photos since I was probably like eight or nine, and … it's kind of become normal, like I never really thought anything of it, like even up to just before this talk, it was kind of just normal? And like, the first video you played, of the advertisements you kinda, like, look at it like 'that's normal'.

Sarah: Yeah.

Peta: Normal, like you don't really think anything of it until you started speaking about it and identifying like, how, um, stereotypical it is? Like, how everyone is expected to look like that, and that's where all the boys get it from, so yeah.

Sarah: And like, every day at school, like *so* many girls are asked by the guys for nudes, and it's like – *(sighs, shakes head)* yeah …

Peta: But it's like normal talk? Like it's at school, you're like – 'Oh, I sent nudes to this guy last night.'

Sarah: It's like, what you send though, it's like girls think it's like a compliment when guys ask them for nudes, like, it's *not* a *compliment*! Like … you don't need to.

Peta: They're just *using* you!

Sarah: Yeah! Exactly!

Mollie: And it's all on, like, you don't have a personality, it's just what you look like.

Sarah: It's all about the body, it's not about who you really *are*.

Mollie: Like, 'sorry if you're a good person, but you don't look that good, so I'm not gonna talk to you'.

Sarah: And like, if we do something that the guys don't like, or if they ask us to do something that we don't wanna do, and we say *no*, they just, like *abuse* us, and it's – ugh. *(Sigh.)*

Peta: And … they go to their friends, and they're like, oh, don't talk to this girl, *she* won't send you nudes, she's –

Sarah: 'She'll dob on you! She'll snitch on you!'

Peta: 'She's a snitch', yeah, like, 'just don't talk to *her*', like, ugh.

Mollie: And then you're just classified as frigid, and a prude, and all of this, and the rumours …

Peta: *(bitterly)* It's so fu – yeah.

Interviewer: So how would you stand up to boys now, that were demanding pictures and treating you bad now?

Sarah: I would just say –

Peta: We've got a personality too! *(Laughs.)*

Mollie: With – there's brains, too, like …

Sarah: Yeah, like – no, I'm not gonna send you a picture of my body, just to please you! Like, I'm my own person. I'm gonna do what *I* want.

Peta: And we have the right to be, like – to keep this to ourselves.

Sarah: Yeah!

Peta: And till we feel like, we can share it with you, *if* we were close, but not just because you're just another popular guy that wants to see us naked, like *(laughs)*.

Sarah: And what you were saying about the *good* guys, like I'll admit, I've always gone for the hot skater boy who's a real shitty person, and not gone for like – the good guys …?

Mollie: And now you just like – you *can't* pick it, cos you're *always* suspicious, you're like …

Peta: You don't know like, if you can trust …

Sarah: And we're just used to being just treated like that.

Peta: Yeah.

Mollie: You don't know *who* you can trust.

Peta: It's your property!

Sarah: Yeah!

Peta: And … recently, someone has screenshotted mine and shown *everyone!*

Sarah: The *whole* school.

Peta: Yeah …

Sarah: And us as girls, it might be frowned upon that we've sent them, but we feel *so pressured* to send them, because if we don't –

Mollie: It's gonna backfire on us.

Sarah: All the guys are gonna abuse us at school. They'll be like 'Oh, she's a prude, oh she's a frigid, oh, she won't do anything …' like, I'm – I'm *allowed* to not do anything! Like, ugh … *(shakes head).*

Interviewer: So what are you gonna do from now on?

Sarah: NOPE! *(Stop hand out.)*

Peta: NO!

Mollie: Sorry!

Sarah: Noooooo! Sorry!

Peta: Hundred per cent! No way!

Sarah: Yep.

Will these girls feel like they can take charge? And are the boys also willing to look at their behaviour? What does the increased sexualisation of younger kids' life space mean for their happiness, and their chances of making good relationships with the opposite sex? And what about the girls who never get to question this role that they have now had put upon them – as homemade porn providers for mid-teen boys?

Nude pics are not a 'sin'. Many adult couples separated by military service or work send erotic pictures to each other. Girls I've talked to in cultures that forbid contact with boys use erotic selfies as part of their courtship, a new variation on the timeless challenge of circumventing parental control! Love is love. But coercion, betrayal, blackmail and shaming around looks and sexuality are very common risks, and the endless comparisons and self-loathing for not measuring up, in every sense, gives it all a very dark side. The girls above are on to this.

Nobody knows all the answers, but it's a conversation worth having with your own daughters and sons. Not judgemental and preachy but just – how does this affect you? Does it make things go well, or badly? Is it harmless, or does it poison things between boys and girls? What are you going to do to make it safe and okay for yourself? And the timeless, powerful message, 'you don't have to do what you don't feel right about'.

How Happy Sexuality Grows By Itself

Let's talk about how it's meant to be. Left to themselves, all young people grow in sexual awareness as puberty wakes them to this new phase of life. It happens slowly, there is a natural reticence or embarrassment that keeps things at a manageable pace.

Just one example of this is that pre-teen and mid-teen girls are often crazy about boy bands or singers who are not sexual in any way, perhaps because this allows a manageability and gentleness in their feelings that lets them feel safe and private.

Girls go from barely tolerating boys in their pre-teens, to finding them interesting but annoying in mid-teens, to gradually finding one or two boys they can relate to enjoyably as good friends as they mature. With any luck, they are able to mix in groups and get more practiced at talking, and check out boys' different characters under a range of circumstances. If they encounter a boy who is funny and kind, able to have a conversation, who doesn't put them or other people down, they may find themselves wanting to pair up and 'go out'.

THE THREE L'S

It's not unusual to be attracted to someone you don't even like, who you would hate to be around. Hormones are like that sometimes. It helps to teach your daughter about the 'three L's': liking, loving and lusting – each of which is quite different. Feeling all three towards one person is what we all hope for, but at the very least we need to know which is which. Confusing lust for love, loving for liking, or liking for lust, all create serious problems. Mothers and fathers can talk about these things in a lighthearted but serious way; girls will need to have a handle on this as it will hugely affect their success at having happy relationships.

When relationships begin, they do so with a lot of caution and testing out. In fact young love is all about exploration, two people gradually unfolding their intimacy as trust grows. It's one of the sweetest times of life, you feel intensely alive and the world seems like a beautiful place.

This is where the sexualisation of kids does most harm. Hammered by media about the need to be sexy, seeing role-models on TV and in movies who separate sex from any kind of relationship aspects, believing that sex is the way to get love, kids now behave not as they *want*, from their inner signals, but *as they feel they should*.

They believe that if they don't deliver, their partner will go elsewhere. When they have sex they are not relaxed or excited, but deeply anxious about how they are 'performing', wondering how they compare to others, and what tricks they are supposed to carry out. A part of life that is meant to be beautiful and life changing has been stolen from this generation. It's a terrible loss.

When interviewed by researchers, girls revealed that much of the sex they were having was in order to keep boys happy. Many found it empty or unsatisfying. Like the 'lie back and think of England' attitudes of a century ago, these girls are resigned to sex being a necessity. Many girls drink a lot of alcohol on nights out with boys just to make it easier, less personal.

THE FACTS

When researchers at Melbourne's Latrobe University carried out their recurring large-scale survey of teenage sexuality, in 2002 and again in 2008, they found something quite alarming. It galvanised those of us who work with teens, and shocked us. The survey found that the percentage of girls who had had sex with multiple partners, while still at school, had *doubled in six years*.[5] Taken across a wider timescale – going back 30 years – that group had grown *from about four per cent to 20 per cent of all girls, and showed no sign of slowing down*. By the time you read this, it will likely be even higher. Multiple partners was defined as three or more. By the age of 17.

Having sex with lots of different partners is not good for your body. While the use of condoms has greatly improved, many girls are on the pill and so don't see the need. Girls are now suffering soaring levels of infections, including chlamydia, which may affect their fertility, and the upsurge of oral sex is leading to a far greater incidence of mouth and throat cancers.

Preventing our daughters from being brainwashed down this road of 'too sexy too soon' has to start early, if possible. The media that comes into your house is a great place to begin.

RELATIONSHIPS – HOW YOUNG IS TOO YOUNG?

The most important message of human development is that you can't jump stages. You can't put the roof on until you've built the walls. We mess up girls when we race them into needs and behaviours that they are not yet neurologically ready for. Most 14- to 18-year-old girls are still forming their identity. Imagine if a 15-year-old gets into an intense relationship with a boy. At this age, she is not yet sure who she is, and so there is a strong chance that she will look to the boy to 'define her' (and vice versa).

She is not yet very secure, so she may cling, fret and worry that he won't like her. Any sign of disinterest will put her in a spin. She won't clearly know what she likes and wants other than what he likes and wants. If he is the same age, he might have the same problem. If he is older, he will find it hard not to automatically call the shots and develop a power relationship where he decides everything that happens. (Girls who lack good fathering often mix up father needs with boyfriend needs, and get into this kind of relationship.)

Girls of 14 or 16 often have boyfriends. It's nice to have someone special in your life, but it's also emotionally hazardous, and not likely to last very long. If it becomes sexual, it can break hearts very easily, and leave baggage for future relationships. Taking it slow is a really good idea.

BEING SMART ABOUT BOYS – THE TALK YOU HAVE TO HAVE

There's a conversation every parent needs to have with their daughter, and it's not the one you think. When we were kids, it was the 'don't get pregnant' talk, but this one is just as important – 'What kind of boy is worth spending your time with, and what kind should you give a big miss?' Talking woman to woman or dad to daughter about this kind of thing is vital, as it gets her brain engaged, and in teenage love that can be a part of the anatomy that is often neglected! Ideally these conversations happen bit by bit over many years, but they come into focus when all of a sudden boys go from irritating to fascinating, and it all begins!

There are two discussions really – what *does* make a good boyfriend (or girlfriend if she is same-sex attracted) and what *doesn't*. What are the definite warning signs to avoid? You know your girl best, so the following are just ideas to get you started. But the main thing is to bring it up in casual ways when the time is right. Don't preach, don't lecture, make it about asking her views. Listen, explore and talk about real world examples. And only very cautiously add your thoughts and experiences! Too many girls today have bruising or even dangerous relationships with messed-up boys. Your daughter doesn't need to be one of them.

The Bottom Line

At the heart of every person is a core attitude to other human beings. They are either respectful of others, or they are not. So there really are two kinds of boy/man (though since we are talking about teens, they are learning which to be, and are allowed to make mistakes). Well-raised and well-loved boys relate to girls as equals with their own needs, feelings and views. They seem to know that if they are honest and vulnerable relationships can grow and thrive. They are tentative but steady, fun and positive to be around.

And then there are the other kind of boy/man, and we all know what they are like. This kind of boy doesn't know how to relate equally, or has only ever seen role models who don't, and so tries to control others using whatever means he can – emotional, physical, financial. He can be charming, but he can't deal with an independent-minded female. It makes him feel insecure. Having a boyfriend like this may start well but rapidly becomes an unpleasant and stressful time. If a boy doesn't make your daughter happy, then he is probably one of these. Power and control are terrible things to have in a relationship. These boys haven't grown up enough and need to go away and practise.

Of course sexual attraction is a big part of teen relating on both sides, but a well-loved boy brings his heart along too. He values closeness and trust and he rises to the challenge of a different being with her own mind. A boy who only wants, to speak plainly, to 'get into her pants' can act tender, interested, charming and romantic. For a while. As long as things go to his timetable. Love is a dance, and if he doesn't know this then pain will follow.

The Partner You Want

You and your daughter won't have trouble listing the qualities that make a good man. (You could also think about good men that you both know, and what it is that makes them good.) Here are a few to get you started.

- *Optimistic and patient.* Watch what happens when things don't go to plan. How do they react to setbacks? Do they have temper tantrums, or go sulky and uncommunicative? Or can they hang in there and keep learning and growing?
- *Good-hearted and kind.* If they complain about former girlfriends, or are mean about people and badmouth them, then that mean side will one day come to focus on you. Of course, if they put you down for your looks, ideas, friends, family, or anything, or worse still, they are ever rough or violent or shout at you, *leave*. Clean break. End of story.

- *Free of addictions.* A very good indicator of a person who is deeply stressed, damaged or affected by trauma is their relationship to substances. Smoking (in this day and age), drinking more than small amounts socially or smoking dope more than very occasionally can all indicate someone who is not coping with life very well.
- *Not jealous or possessive.* If you spend time with your friends, or talk to another guy who is not a romantic interest but just a friend, how do they react? A secure partner will be happy to see you happy.
- *Funny, creative, full of life.* Often girls are surprised that the good-looking hunk they have lusted after is actually really boring – strong and silent can just mean there is not a lot going on! Or that what is going on is so buried you'll never find it. A partner ought to be an individual, and bring out your own sense of spontaneity and wildness too.
- *Reliable.* No matter how much fun, he needs backbone too. He does what he says. Keeps his promises. Shows up on time. Doesn't wimp out when it's tiring or hard. Makes sacrifices for bigger goals. You are safe with him. Those are huge things for the long haul. Life is not always a party, and strong needs strong.

Mr Wrong

- *Intensity* is always a warning sign. He doesn't need to get to know you because he has you imagined already! Someone saying they love you straight away is a well-known danger sign – you've become his fantasy woman and will be expected to follow the script. Obsession is the most dangerous trait in a partner because it means their grip on reality is not strong.
- *He's incredibly good-looking,* buff and groomed. That all takes time, and probably means he's a complete narcissist who spends all his energy on himself, and you are just going to be an accessory.

- *He's edgy and exciting.* (Translation – he's got anxiety issues which he manages with smoking or drinking, and authority issues which will end up with a road accident or jail.)
- *He really needs me,* and tells me I am everything to him. (Translation – he's emotionally needy, which translates into being a manipulator, having tantrums, sulking, and when he is really upset, one day beating you up.)
- *He is strong, silent and wonderful.* (Translation – he's got no emotional intelligence and doesn't know how to share, be vulnerable or be open hearted.) So, boring. A good partner is someone who can make mistakes, talk things through, change and grow. And does change – you don't find yourself fixing the same problem over and over.

Ask your daughter which qualities are her most important in a partner? Which are an absolute deal-breaker? And keep it real! Adolescence is about learning from our mistakes. You won't be able to protect your daughter (or son) from some heartbreak, but girls' hearts are actually strong and heal very well. The main thing is that she can recognise early when she is In a rubbish relationship, and not spend years of wasted time. By showing your daughter you trust her judgement, you make it more likely she will hear her own alarm bells and move on to the kind of boy every girl deserves. The happy, equal, respectful kind.

Stopping the Toxic Flood

Though we don't like to admit it, we human beings are 'herd animals'. Being intensely social, we take our cues from those around us as to what is normal, but today, those cues come not so much from real people as from media: TV, movies, music videos and magazines. In the last 50 years, and especially the last ten, we have shifted from spending hours a day with family, relatives and friends to spending much more time isolated in our houses or rooms. Some commentators believe that today's girls only have *one-fifth as much time* with caring older adults compared to 50 years ago.[6] When Grandma lived down the road and several aunties or friends of Mum lived in the same small town, girls had lots of 'wise woman' talk in their lives.

Today that's all changed. We watch *Neighbours* instead of talking to our real neighbours, and *Friends* instead of spending time with real friends. (TV has almost *become* our family; jovial, non-threatening men and reassuringly maternal women join us at breakfast, just as Mum and Dad once did in the old days.)

We adults use TV for entertainment, but our kids use it for quite a different purpose: *to find out what is normal behaviour.* Of course, what they see is far from normal. With each passing year, TV programming has to be more and more sexually explicit, more violent, more rude and abusive, more emotionally intense, to hold our interest. The characters have to be more ravishingly good looking and 'hot' to keep people watching. So what is normal on TV is wildly at odds with real life.

Many kids' favourite shows are 'reality' programmes. These often feature immature young adults in situations of contrived flirtation, rejection and hurt, bullying and exclusion. Kids know all about rejection and exclusion, and so they watch, mesmerised. They see competitive and nasty behaviour, selfishness and cruelty portrayed as normal. They think the world must be like this – a big and heartless place where no one cares. If you are not pretty enough or sexy enough, you won't be 'chosen'.

There are many other changes. When we were kids, children's viewing was very defined. Today it all blurs – horrific news items interrupt afternoon viewing, crass and offensive behaviour is in so-called 'family' shows. (A classic is *Two and a Half Men*, which has a child included in its cast and the running joke is his exposure to the sexual exploits of the 'grown-ups'.)

Can't We Just Teach Them to Resist?

It's not that there is any one terrible instance of media harm, it's the relentless, damaging flood of material. Inch by inch, kids are progressively brainwashed about what it is normal to think, feel, look like and do. They can be helped to resist some of this, *but it's really hard work*. The experts who advise us to 'discuss the media with your children, help them to deconstruct the messages, and be media aware' are not wrong, and we should do this. But so much of the effect is unconscious, and it just keeps coming.

TV and magazine ads have an especially insidious influence on girls. The market in selling useless things to pre-teen and mid-teen girls is worth billions of dollars each year, across the globe. These purchases are things that girls never needed or thought of in earlier generations – make-up, skin and hair products, fashion and footwear that piles up in cupboards. Twenty years ago a teenage girl would go downtown happily in jeans and a clean T-shirt. Today it takes an hour of anxious preparation before she will go out in public. Even toys and games for little girls are about fashion, beauty, modelling and being sexy.

The aim of advertising is to attack your mental health – to worry you and make you discontent. If you want to sell products to a girl, whether she is four or 14, *you first have to make her insecure* – about her looks, friends, clothes, weight, skin and hair. Everything about her is an opportunity to fail.

TV, magazines, billboards and music videos pour this 'lookism' message onto girls wherever they turn. The result: appearance has become the primary concern of children who should have never given it a second thought.

Clothes were once worn to keep the wind out! Now mothers complain that it's almost impossible to buy girls' clothing for pre-teens or teens that isn't revealing or, as one put it, slutty. I couldn't help smiling when a colleague who counsels sex-workers told me there was real annoyance among her clients that they no longer could be identified in the streets because *17-year-olds dressed and looked just like them.*

NIP AND TUCK

At a recent talk I gave in Sydney, Australia, a group of young women doctors cornered me after the show. They told me that they were receiving frequent requests from teenage girls *for plastic surgery on their labia*. These girls had seen porn movies or photos and were deeply concerned that they looked 'untidy' and they wanted to be tidied up. The American College of Obstetricians has been concerned enough at this trend to issue a warning on side effects including nerve damage, painful coitus, tissue adhesion and painful scars. Some thoughtful websites and publications have appeared to show girls the huge variety of how labia can look, with the aim of persuading them to like their bodies they way they are.

THE PEOPLE WE WORRY ABOUT

There is a pattern that a great many families have with television – *they have it on all the time*. The first to wake up turns it on, the last to go to bed turns it off. In these families, some distinct things happen:

1. Nobody ever has a good conversation – either long, or deep – because you can't when people have divided attention. So it just doesn't happen. 'Always On' families don't talk much. They grumble a lot though.
2. The kids absorb thousands of messages, bewildering, random, scary, distorted, artificial and just plain wrong, about life and the world. People who watch a lot of TV are found to be much more anxious, depressed, fearful, inattentive and powerless than those who don't. And as many a parent has tried to explain to a terrified three-year-old who just saw something they shouldn't, 'it isn't real'. But to them it's more real than life. After all, it's on the telly.

Would you invite scary adults into your house to make your children anxious and pressure them to buy things they don't need for problems they don't have? As a parent, you are in charge of the emotional safety of your home. You have to decide what comes through your door, and through your television. TV wants to own your daughter's mind; you mustn't let it.

What Can We Do?

Let's tackle the easy issues first. Television stands out like the Mount Everest of media intrusion into children's lives. While the internet takes over more in the teen years, TV is your child's teacher for thousands of hours of their formative years. It's there in the corner of the living room, sometimes in many other rooms as well. It's like a third parent.

What does it teach? Researchers have identified six key messages:

1. *Your looks are the most important thing about you.*
2. *Your physical characteristics (shape, weight, skin, hair, teeth, colour, smell) are NEVER EVER good enough.*
3. *Sex is something that you exchange, for love and attention, or for power. It's primarily a currency.*
4. *It's normal and fine to have sex with people you don't even know, or especially like.*
5. *The world is a scary, lonely, dangerous and competitive place. Better get going – you might lose the race.*
6. *The answer to all life's problems is to buy something.*

If you agree with these messages, that's fine. You, your partner and the TV are all of one accord. If you don't agree, though, you have to act.

Step One – No TV in Bedrooms

All the research from around the world shows that kids with their own TV see far more unsuitable material, and do so without the awareness or discussion with you, their parents.

This causes harm to them. They are much more prone to anxiety, they have measurably poorer sleep, and do less well at school. If you have TVs in your kids' bedrooms, take them away now!

Step Two – Consciously Decide What You View

You need to decide where your family will be on the TV-using spectrum. Some families *don't even have TV*. About 3 per cent of families make this choice at present, and it's growing.[7] Their kids are more creative, settled, do better at school and have far wider interests.

Next, some families have taken the American Pediatric Association's guidelines on board and don't have TV for the under threes. (The APA found that TV has no benefits for and in fact causes significant harm to babies and toddlers, diminishing their language development and stressing them, reducing their activity levels, even affecting their vision by being at a fixed focal length when toddlers need to be looking far and near.)[8]

Some families have TV but use only DVDs and pre-recorded favourite shows, discovering that small kids often love to watch the same shows many times, getting familiar with the dialogue and songs. This way they can eliminate ads, the jumpy interruptions, and scary news breaks or promos that occur on almost all stations.

Many families, with kids at any age, have started to have their TV on only for specific shows, chosen by each child, perhaps for half an hour a day each. It's never just left running.

Magazines

The same goes for magazines, especially fashion magazines and girls' magazines, which are bursting at the seams with ads for make-up and clothes. Don't buy them. There are some great alternatives.

Girls' magazines have occasional bursts of trying to clean up their act. One has recently stopped using airbrushed images; another stopped running its 'model quest'. Then brought it back. Sometimes these publications run worthwhile articles and have a good advice column, but their reason for existing is advertising, so they aren't going to stop their primary harm, which is making girls not like themselves *as they are*. That wouldn't sell much merchandise. Advertising is the misery industry – it makes you less happy with yourself and your life. *Girls really don't need any help with this.*

Then there's the content. Which boys are hot. How to *be* hot. Hotness competitions. We could go on, but you get the idea.

To sum up, you can choose the media that comes into your home, and you can start right away. If your daughters are little, you can make a huge difference. If they are older, it's still not too late. You can also do the other things in this book: raise their sense of being loved and special, with an identity built on what they DO not how they look. You can build their sense of community and belonging with other adults and activities so there are lots of buffers to their believing in themselves. It all works together, you just have to have your eyes open.

GIRLS AND DESIRE – WHAT SHOULD YOU TEACH YOUR DAUGHTER?

Reading the many discussions of teenage girls and sex, you could start to feel that it's all about trouble. So it's extremely important to keep a true perspective – that sex is a beautiful, exciting and health-giving thing, and that girls ought to own it, enjoy it and revel in it.

Girls have every bit as much desire and yearning as their boy counterparts. We parents, especially mothers, need to tell our girls long before the anxieties have time to get a hold that sex is great and they are going to love it.

Deborah Tolman, at the Center for Research on Women, in the USA, carried out some stunning interviews with girls for her book *Dilemmas of Desire*.[9] She found a concerning thing, that when teen girls talked about sex, *they too emphasised the negatives*. More than that, they frequently sounded weak and passive in describing sexual experiences they had already had. This could be best summed up in the phrase 'It just happened'. Being with a boy they are not really sure they like, having a bit too much to drink, and sex 'happening' seems almost the norm. This was how they experienced it – not a lot of choice, not a lot of desire, no real intention and no real sense of 'agency' (being the active one and seeking and getting a wonderful time). There wasn't a lot of 'I wanted ...' or 'I loved ...' or 'I enjoyed ...' in their language.

This really needs to be improved. As much as adults worry about teenagers being too sexual, there is a paradoxical thing that Tolman and others, including myself, have come to believe:

Girls who are in touch with their own sexual desires, and comfortable to acknowledge and express them, are better able to choose whether or not to have sex, who with, and under what circumstances.

Too often in the past, parents and society have sent a message that there are only two kinds of girls: 'bad' girls who presumably love sex, and 'good' girls who presumably don't. This sets girls up for having a bad time. If a girl feels desire, she might label this as bad, and suppress it. Or a girl wanting to be rebellious might have sex when really she doesn't want to – it's just a way to make a statement or get some affirmation that she is interesting and worthwhile. It all gets very messy.

Talking about this might not be where every mother-daughter's relationship is at, but it's worth working for. Some teenagers don't like talking about sex with parents, but we need to make sure someone is talking to them. Sometimes aunties or older women friends can affirm this more comfortably for girls than their mums can. Tolman said in her book that, 'Every girl I interviewed said that no adult woman had ever talked to her before about sexual desire and pleasure "like this", that is, so overtly, specifically, or in such depth.' Perhaps we should.

In a Nutshell

- Mainstream media, half by accident, half by intent, is making sex seem compulsory for girls at increasingly younger ages.
- It damages teen girls by sexualising them when they are not equipped or ready.
- Young love is being trashed by making it performance-laden, shallow and rushed.
- Girls are now much more anxious about their looks, clothes and fitting in.
- Because this starts very young, we can make a big difference by not having much or any television in small children's lives. We can choose which magazines and other media to buy. We can talk to our daughters and foster an empowered and conscious sense of their sexuality that is special and personal – not a commodity.
- All the positive things you do to give your daughter connections and interests will set her free to have a happy and enthusiastic sex life when she is ready, and by her own choice.

Chapter 9

Mean Girls

Bullying is in the news, it seems to be happening everywhere – in the adult world as well as in the world of children. Experts do not think it's an epidemic, but rather that at last people have really had enough of it and are speaking up. Bullying is being called what it is, and that's the first step to ending it.

Among girls, bullying is most often done in non-physical ways – name-calling, spreading nasty rumours online, excluding or embarrassing a girl by pulling faces or rolling eyes to make her feel stupid. This is sometimes called 'relational aggression', which is to say that just because you aren't getting hit, doesn't mean it doesn't hurt.

Physical bullying still happens too, especially among younger girls, and of course from boys. Bullying at any one time affects one in five children worldwide, and is so severe in some cases that it has caused suicides, shootings and knifings, but above all real misery for millions of boys and girls.[1] It is something we have to address.

Small But Strong

This story was told to me by a mother in Wellington, New Zealand. Her daughter Kiri, aged seven, was the smallest in her class, a lively and quick-minded girl who loved school. One day, Kiri came home very upset. She sobbed in her mother's arms, would not eat her evening meal, but refused to talk about what had made her so unhappy. Then, later that night, she finally told her dad about it.

A much larger girl at school had for several weeks been picking on her, pushing her out of games with her friends and then taking her place. It was annoying, and scary, and more than once the girl had really hurt her arms by squeezing her hard. But the biggest hurt was the feeling of powerless humiliation. That's why she found it so hard to tell her family.

Kiri's dad and mum emailed the head of the school that night, labelling the email as a 'complaint' so that it was formal and would have to be taken notice of. The next day her dad phoned for an appointment and met with the headteacher that same afternoon. The head interviewed each of the girls in that social group to get more of the picture. He then met with the girl who was doing the bullying and Kiri together, and asked the girl to apologise and promise to stop. Rather graciously, Kiri said that it had not happened as much lately.

Under this much scrutiny, and with the impact of the interview (which was done in a thoughtful way and not punitive or angry in tone), the bullying stopped.

It didn't escape Kiri's parents that it was her dad she had told about her problem. Kiri was one of five children and her dad was quite a busy man, but he decided this was a kind of reaching out for him, and so he decided to do more with his daughter. He and Kiri started going swimming together at a centre nearby. This was not something he or she had ever done before, and they both really enjoyed it. She gained confidence in deep water, and began to enjoy swimming at school too because she was now more familiar with it. She also really loved the time with her dad. Kiri's sense of self-worth visibly grew.

In short, the response of everyone turned the situation into one that increased Kiri's confidence and turned the crisis into an opportunity to grow.

It Takes Three

There are always three parts to a bullying situation. First, the perpetrator. This is usually someone who is feeling badly about themselves, who gets to feel better by passing on their pain to someone else. Research into children who bully has found that they suffer more from depression and are also more prone to suicide in later life. The girl who bullied Kiri was a bit of a loner who was having a difficult time at home.[2] It's likely this girl envied Kiri for her happiness and circle of friends, but also since she was small, saw her as someone she could easily push around.

The second part is the victim. Kiri did not deserve to be bullied, but she gained strength and it's likely she would speak up more for herself in future. The evidence suggests that it doesn't work to 'hit back' with bullies – often they are bigger or there are a group of them[3] – but verbally responding, being angry, and of course asking for help, being definite about your rights to be not pushed around, all help.

Finally, there are the bystanders. If they speak up and object to the bullying, stand alongside the victim, and if need be tell others what is happening, bullying often stops. This is hard because sometimes girls feel that if they do this they will become the next victim. Talk to your daughter about how important it is to protect others who are less strong or confident, and tell her what she can say to intervene, things like, 'Hey, that's not fair', 'She's my friend, leave her alone', 'Stop being stupid. You are hurting her', along with some confident body language.

In Kiri's case the school responded well and gave the situation time and energy. The head of the school saw it as a chance to improve the connectedness between himself and the children, create a safer environment, and do it in a non-punishing way. The staff also discussed how they could meet the needs of the bullying girl too, as she was clearly having a hard time in her life.

The three-part solution is important. The 'victim' becomes more confident, sometimes by receiving more long-term support and finding ways to develop her sense of power. In Kiri's case this came from more one-to-one time with her dad. The 'bully' becomes more aware of others' feelings, but also of her own feelings, which may be in a lot of pain and need some real care. And the community around the problem – the school, or family or workplace – is changed by people talking more honestly about what is happening and not just ignoring it.

Speaking Up

Rosalind Wiseman is world famous for her book about bullying and girls, called *Queen Bees and Wannabes*. Rosalind is like the auntie you always wanted – friendly, straight talking, and absolutely clear in her advice. She taught self-defence classes to girls for many years, and the girls often shared with her their social and personal problems with bullying and cliques. She now campaigns full time 'for dignity in how people treat each other'.

Her advice is extraordinarily clear ...

To a 13-year-old teased by a boy (using obscene language) about her breast size, she says 'write down exactly what he says to you, and where and when, and your feelings about that. Get it all down. Take it to the smartest and best school counsellor or teacher and administrator that you know at your school and ask them to help. You absolutely have the right to not be talked to like that'.[4]

An aunt and mother ask her about sexy text messages that their 14-year-old girl has been sending to boys. Wiseman dismisses the privacy concerns completely. 'You own the mobile phone and pay the bills. You own that phone. But more than that, texting is not private. Anyone can read texts or pass them on. If you want to be private, use a diary. Texting is public behaviour and parents need to know about it.'

While being very clear about the need to intervene, Wiseman is empathic with both sides of the situation. She points out that the girl wants to sound sexy, interesting and grown-up to these boys. From her viewpoint, that's what she is doing. To the boys it sounds like she is advertising her availability to actually do those things she is texting. Maybe this is true, or not, but it's a parent's job to intervene protectively. Parents have a better handle on consequences. They can do this sensitively and kindly, but with a clear boundary.

The Importance of Bystanders

Wiseman's work has also underscored the importance of bystanders. In 2011 she helped make a documentary for the NBC television programme *Dateline*. In a powerful and revealing experiment, teenage girls were brought into the studio and left in a large room to choose clothes, supposedly for a segment about fashion choices.

Unknown to the others, three of the girls in each group were professional actors. On cue, two of them began to bully the third (in one instance about her weight, in another, about her choice of clothes) to see how the other girls would react – would they help, or would they join in? Meanwhile, their parents watched from another room.

What unfolded was powerful and moving – since almost all of us have been bullied in our lives, it's hard to watch without being affected. In some of the instances, the bystanders spoke up. One girl in particular was wonderful to watch, she simply would NOT allow the actors to speak rudely to the third girl. But in other instances, girls who were nervous and unsure of themselves actually joined in the laughter.

(A typical strategy of bullies is to recruit others into their 'gang' as a prelude to picking on someone else, and it's easy for insecure girls to fall in with this out of their own fear of exclusion.)

Their mothers cringed as they watched on a monitor in the next room, and saw their daughters joining in the mockery and not doing anything to stop it.

But the final incident was the most touching. In the final group to go through the experiment, one girl could be seen on camera silently walking away and weeping. The film's producers immediately stopped and intervened. It emerged that this girl was being actively bullied at school *in real life*, by both girls and boys, who targeted her for being poor. She was physically afraid each day she went to school. *She had not been able to tell her mother*, because it would make her mum feel worse about their low income. It was a powerful moment as the mothers returned to the room and it was all discussed. Rosalind Wiseman helped this girl (privately after the sessions) to learn to deal with her attackers, and the programme reported that she had successfully stood up to a boy and a girl who had been ringleaders at her school. It was a stark reminder of how cruelty arises so easily, and needs to be dealt with – by bystanders first, but by adults as well – in sending clear signals and always following through.

Everyone Experiences Bullying

It's important to understand that we ALL are bullies sometimes, we are all victims sometimes, and we are all bystanders sometimes who do or do not intervene. It's a natural and important part of getting along with others that we learn to assert what we need, express opinions and stand up for ourselves.

It's important for your daughter to have some things to say when others push her around. 'I don't like you doing that. You need to stop.' A worldwide programme called Rock and Water was developed after bullies actually killed a boy in Holland, and there was an outcry to make changes in schools. Rock and Water teaches kids skills such as how to stand at their full height, make strong eye contact, and walk away while looking back at the aggressor. It is a complete programme in self-confidence and physical safety, but the essence of its message is 'standing strong.'

Teach your daughter to be able to say, 'That's bullying, that's not right.' Of course that won't always stop what's happening, but it's the first step. Name what is happening. 'You're bullying her/me, that isn't right/that's so unfair/that's so uncool.' If bullying continues, go and get help. Tell your daughter clearly that she has a right to be safe and respected, and make it real. Follow up with the school if need be, and don't stay at a school that doesn't take sufficient action. (Your child's school should have a programme addressing bullying, making it clearly understood and identified, so everyone knows what to do and how to get help.)

The world has bullied women and girls as a group for thousands of years. Standing up for yourself as a girl is part of a historic change too. That's another good reason to do it.

GIRLS DO BULLYING DIFFERENTLY

Most of us, when we think of bullying, picture the physical kind. Being punched or pushed around or having your property damaged. Among girls though, bullying is often more about using social weapons, and it's feelings that get hurt.

What psychologists call 'relational bullying' is harder to spot (and harder for parents or teachers to control). Relational bullying includes things like exclusion, sarcasm, gossiping and spreading rumours. It may take the form of a girl acting in a friendly way and then withdrawing or using that to control or exploit. Because girls are often more sensitive to social nuances, relational bullying can do serious harm. It often leads to depression, acute anxiety and, if it goes on for a long time, self-harm and even suicide. It's a huge thing in the lives of many girls.

The first thing to do as a parent is always to be available and willing to talk. If you have a close relationship with your daughter, you will know when something is wrong. And she is more likely to tell you about any hurts or harms she is encountering. This means that in the primary school and teenage years mums and dads have to avoid being too busy, so that you have casual times with her many times a week where you keep abreast of her world and her life.

This, along with the presence of other adult women in her world – aunties, family friends, grandmothers – and of course dad or grandad, also makes her more resilient to peer-group nastiness. She knows she is worthwhile and interesting and loved. So some kid being mean at school doesn't carry as much weight.

Family therapists have a rule of thumb about peer-group pressure. While all kids are affected by their peer groups, some are more intensely concerned and influenced by them. Peer-group approval feels like life-and-death to these youngsters. These are most often the kids who are not close to their same-sex parent – so for girls, their mother. Girls with a poor relationship with their mum put more of their needs for emotional support and affirmation onto their friends instead. But the peer group is often poor at nurturing, and in fact may take advantage of her. So it sets her up for an even worse time. If your daughter seems obsessed with her peer group, wanting to do and be exactly what they dictate, then check – does she have alternative sources of self-esteem – friends or activities away from that group, or enough adults, including you – who she gets to spend time with?

To spot relational bullying, watch for changes in her mood or habits. A usually cheerful girl who becomes silent, withdrawn or falsely cheerful can be the clue that something is amiss. Choose your moment to talk to her, when no one else is around and she is relaxed, and when you have time to hear a long outpouring, if that's what is needed. But don't delay.

Just naming the existence of 'relational bullying' is a big start. The most common forms (you can check this list with your daughter) are the following four:

1. excluding someone from parties and other social activities
2. mocking, teasing or saying something mean but following it with 'just joking'
3. starting rumours and gossip in person, online, or by cell phone
4. threatening to take away friendship if someone doesn't toe the line.[5]

Or she may add others she has seen or experienced. Kids from caring homes are often baffled at the meanness of some children they encounter even in kindergarten or pre-school, or think something is wrong with them. Some parents even teach their soft-hearted kids to speak up loudly, stick their jaw out, and rehearse things to say to let kids know, 'don't do that to me!'

If kids clearly know these behaviours are wrong and harmful, then they will feel more empowered to move away from girls who behave in these ways and choose better friends. And they can speak out to those boys or girls who might be doing it, clearly describing what is happening. 'I feel bad when you act friendly one minute, then go all cold. Is there a reason you are doing that?' And when someone says 'just joking' they can ask, 'so when is the funny part?'

Cyberbullying

With the advent of social media – Facebook, texting, email and Twitter – a whole new kind of bullying has been made possible. Sending horrible texts, spreading rumours or cruel comments online has become widespread.

The worst thing is that girls who have their mobile phone or computer in their bedroom feel they should check on what's happening when they are at home or late at night when they're in bed. In the 'good old days' before computers or iPhones, home was at least a haven of peace until the next day. The result is a lot of stress and sleeplessness.

It's a good idea not to allow digital media in bedrooms, and have a rule that all members of the family charge and leave their phones in the kitchen each night. But once again, messaging of a threatening or ugly kind should not just be kept private. Not responding to minor examples may cause it to stop, but if it persists or is especially nasty, it needs to be taken up with the school or the provider. Also you don't have to make yourself available to it – change privacy settings, 'defriend' people who aren't being friendly, change your number, or get a new email address.

In an excellent movie about girls growing up, *The Descendants*, starring George Clooney, a 'distant dad' is forced to care for his daughters after his wife has a boating accident. Early in the movie, his younger daughter is involved in sending mean texts to a girl at school about her weight. The girl's mother, a feisty Hawaiian, demands an apology from daughter and father. The cyberbullying was done out of a kind of blindness to its consequence – it just felt to her like a joke, shared by a group of friends. She realises the harm she has done, and is somewhat ashamed, but it helps that her father also is embarrassed and shows it, and is keen to fix it up.

Sometimes talking to the person doing it, or their parents, can be done in a reasonable and friendly way by you or by the school, and it can bring about some growing up.

Where Is This Meanness Coming From?

Maggie Hamilton, an Australian writer about girls' lives, has a very good explanation of how meanness has arisen in girl culture today. Maggie believes that girls who are deeply stressed by the pressure to conform to our highly competitive and insecure world, begin to operate in survival mode, constantly anxious and hyper-vigilant.[6] They don't get enough love at home, have grown up too fast, and are constantly on edge. As a result, they do not have the time or place for empathy or kindness.

Bullying expert Kate Hadwen and her team at Edith Cowan University in Perth, Western Australia, surveyed many thousands of children in schools across the state and found that about one in five bullies is not responsive to ordinary appeals to empathy.[7] In other words, ordinary programmes will not work with them. These kids will require long-term intervention, and are at risk of both doing a lot of harm, and ending up in a lot of trouble. This rather chilling fact means that adults have to be willing to intervene, as kids themselves will not be safe unless action is taken long term to monitor the problem.

While the 'mean girls' culture has got a lot of attention it's important to realise that most school environments are not like that at all. When *Queen Bees and Wannabes* became a bestseller, hundreds of girls wrote to Rosalind Wiseman to tell her they recognised exactly the world she described. But then something interesting happened ... Hundreds more girls and women wrote saying that *their girlhood was nothing like this*. It began to be clear that Wiseman was writing about a particular sector of America, and the UK, and Australia, and every developed industrial nation, that was not representative of the whole. At least, not yet.

Girls in these better environments still had friendship groups and some degree of status competition – the popular 'cool' girls, the more study-oriented girls, the gentler more bohemian kids and so on – but they were not by and large mean to each other. And the boundaries were more flexible; you could move about and, more importantly, you could be yourself. It was kinder, and more happy and relaxed.

Often the mean girls are found more at the extremes of society – on the one hand is the more affluent demographic, but also the more competitive one, where parents are financially better off but are time-poor and less engaged. These girls have iPhones and visa cards and sometimes their own cars, but they do not have a whole lot of love. By contrast, some meanness comes from serious poverty and hardship, where parents are too busy or absent, and aggression is a common coping device. But this is not always so, there are poor kids who are also very kind and rich kids who are protective and gentle. There is always freedom to choose what kind of person you will be.

In a Nutshell

- Bullying affects about one in five children – it's way too common and causes a lot of pain.
- Stopping bullying requires change in all three players: victim, perpetrator and bystanders.
- Bystanders are a vital way to prevent bullying – they can make a joke to break up the interaction. Talk to your girl about doing this for other girls.
- Cyberbullying has become a problem because it can be done at a distance. Dealing with it involves shortening that distance by communicating the hurt and concern back to the perpetrator.
- Adults need to know about bullying and to act when it is occurring, but not in a way that makes it worse. Calm, friendly but determined action is best.
- Some girl cultures are mean because of the lack of love in that demographic. There are plenty of girl cultures that are healthy and supportive.

Chapter 10

Bodies, Weight and Food

By Lydia Jade Turner and Sarah McMahon

Does your daughter worry about her weight? Do you worry about yours? You aren't alone, because body image has become a worldwide obsession and people have never been more confused – or unwell. About 15 per cent of all girls and women will experience an eating disorder at some time in their lives – it is a massive epidemic.[1]

Not long ago I listened to two young women presenting a stunning analysis of what the science is telling us about health, food and body size. Lydia Jade Turner and Sarah McMahon have backgrounds in clinical work with eating disorders, but they are also committed to changing the culture around diet obsession, and especially a diet industry that makes matters a whole lot worse. Lydia and Sarah agreed to write this specialist chapter for the book.

A Candle Burning at Both Ends

Most countries around the world are facing a serious public health crisis over body weight, and that crisis has two extremes. On the one hand, approximately one-quarter of school-aged children are reported to be 'overweight' or 'obese'; on the other, the National Eating Disorders Collaboration reports the frightening news that eating disorders have increased two-fold in the past five years.[2] While some parents are being pressured to put their children on diets, others are dealing with the horror of watching their daughters refuse to eat anything at all. The terrifying thing is that none of this is working. Despite all the anti-obesity rhetoric, children are getting fatter, and despite warnings about eating disorders, more girls are falling prey to them. We are doing something wrong.

Leading health experts from many countries now believe that the problem arises from putting our focus on the wrong thing; we shouldn't be focused on weight, because weight is not as important as health. Their research shows that if we shift our focus onto health, and enjoying eating and exercising our bodies, we would be far better off.[3]

Why Dieting Is Harmful

You may be shocked to learn that 50 years of research has come to an astounding conclusion: *dieting hardly ever works*.[4] Approximately 95 per cent of all people who go on diets regain the weight lost within two to five years. There are no diets anywhere that do better than this. How many times have you heard a new diet claiming to be the one that will make you lose kilos if only you buy this book and this product? If this confuses us as adults, imagine what happens if we pass this on to our children?

It does not matter what a company calls its weight-loss approach, none have been shown through sound research to lead to long-term

weight loss for more than a tiny fraction of those who use it. You might have noticed that many diet companies no longer use the word diet, they talk about 'lifestyle' instead. But diets are still what they sell.

The multi-billion-dollar diet industry has a huge advertising presence and your daughter will see the ads everywhere. This decades-long marketing effort has convinced most people of a terrible fallacy – that fat people are fat because they lack the willpower to keep weight off over the long term. We are taught to shun fat people, to be fearful of becoming one of them, or, if we are already fat, to do all that we can to whittle our bodies down to a slimmer physique.

The incredible thing is that after all this marketing and all the government campaigns there is not a single country in the world that has successfully reduced obesity rates.

Healthy eating and regular exercise improves health but do not necessarily lead to significant weight loss. It's more important, and more successful, to focus on being healthy.

THE WAY WE ARE MADE

There's a reason why diets are not successful. Humans evolved for a tough Stone Age environment, when food was often scarce, and so our bodies are wired to protect our healthy weight. When we diet, *our body thinks it's a famine, and triggers mechanisms to try to put the weight back on*. A study in the *New England Journal of Medicine* found the appetite-stimulating hormone, ghrelin, increased in dieters by approximately 20 per cent.[5] Appetite-suppressing hormones such as leptin and peptide YY were also found at unusually low levels. Our metabolic rate also slows if we diet – so that we can conserve weight!

Is the solution to just try, try again? Interestingly, research has found that over time dieting actually makes us fatter. A groundbreaking study by Dr Dianne Neumark-Sztainer, of the University of Minnesota School of Public Health, showed adolescent girls who engage in weight-control behaviours end up significantly heavier than their peers five years later.[6] Another study tracked 15,000 participants aged between nine and 14.[7] It found that 'tweens' and teenagers who were put on diets were significantly more likely to gain weight than those who were not. And worst news of all – dieting is also the biggest predictor of an eating disorder, with one in five obese Australians now found to have eating disorder symptoms, despite maintaining a higher weight.

How Fat-Shaming Just Makes Things Worse

Fat-shaming is often used as a way to try to motivate us to achieve better health. Nothing could be worse. TV shows like *The Biggest Loser* humiliate their fat contestants while reinforcing the stereotype that all fat people are fat due to poor health choices. Yet research shows that being ashamed of one's weight was a risk factor for both those suffering from obesity and eating disorders, while also *reducing the likelihood of a person engaging in regular physical activity*.[8] Given that exercise typically takes place in a public space, it makes sense that people – especially teenage girls – who feel particularly ashamed of the way they look, would not feel comfortable wearing gym clothes or swimsuits or doing anything that draws attention to their bodies.

Bullying under the guise of health is fast becoming a national pastime. This hysteria towards fatness is killing us and our daughters. One study found obese children were 63 per cent more likely to be bullied.[9] While it's understandable that parents wish to help their child escape bullying, putting a child on a diet is not the solution. It makes them feel it's their fault.

School and other health programmes tackling obesity the wrong way may cause great harm. Professor Jennifer O'Dea, of the University of Sydney, found 'health education for child obesity prevention may result in ... unplanned, undesirable and health-damaging effects such as starvation, vomiting, laxative abuse, diuretic and slimming abuse, and cigarette smoking to suppress appetite and as a substitute for eating.'[10] Eating Disorders Victoria (an Australian eating disorder support service) reports 8 per cent of adolescent girls currently smoke to control their weight.[11]

The Other Extreme

When we hear the words 'eating disorder' we most often think of people who are extremely thin. But in fact most eating-disorder sufferers are not emaciated, with those suffering from bulimia or binge-eating disorder often maintaining a 'healthy weight' or higher. Anorexia – not eating to the point of serious weight loss – is certainly not helped by our obsession with weight, and in fact many girls admire and idolise anorexic friends for their assumed iron will and self-control. Emerging research suggests anorexia is a brain disorder exacerbated by starvation.[12] It takes intensive clinical help to overcome the disordered thinking and behaviours, and without this there is a serious risk of damage or death.

Binge eating is a far more common problem. Eating large amounts of food in an intense burst is a natural response to dieting, as the body tries to hold on to fat stores. It turns up the appetite-stimulating hormones and we become highly attuned to food, causing us to become obsessed and distracted with eating. Binge eating is our body's way of trying to help us survive. For reasons not fully understood, the anorexia sufferer's physiology does not 'kick in' to help her survive; many anorexic patients report actually feeling better when they are starving themselves, and that's why it's such a dangerous condition.

What To Do Instead

Our bodies are constantly communicating to us: when we are hungry, we should eat; when we are approaching fullness, stop. Constipation is another signal that tells us we might have insufficient fibre in our diet. Our body has a biological system that internally regulates many facets of our survival – including blood pressure and body temperature, and strives to defend a set-point weight.

Dieting is a terrible trap. Many get caught on a vicious cycle of losing weight in the short term, only to experience a strong preoccupation with food and cravings which in turn leads to weight gain, so then they embark on a diet yet again. Numerous studies have shown weight cycling to be more detrimental to health than maintaining a higher but steady weight, so the idea that one should 'try, try again' is actually a harmful one.[13]

Many health professionals are now ditching weight as an appropriate measure of health and are instead embracing a health-centred approach known as Health At Every Size (HAES). HAES argues that fitness is actually a much more accurate assessment of health than size (except at statistical extremes). Body Mass Index (BMI) is a poor indicator of health. There are other biomarkers that can be used to measure health, such as blood pressure and heart rate. Two key principles are intuitive eating and finding physical movement that is joyful instead of focused on weight loss. Every day we could go to bed feeling good for having engaged in health-giving behaviours, rather than beating ourselves up for not yet being a certain number on the scales.

How You Can Help Your Daughter

1. *Become the role model she needs. If you obsess about weight, so will she. Ditch the diet talk, don't watch those TV shows and don't have fashion or weight-loss magazines around the house. Don't even think about going on a 'diet'.*

2. *Don't have soft drinks in the fridge. They confuse thirst with hunger, and even the diet brands have unhealthy chemicals in them. Have a jug of cold water.*

3. *Have meals together at a table, with no TV playing. When you watch TV while eating, you don't notice the food properly, or really taste it. And you don't notice when you've had plenty. Noticing you are full happens a few minutes after you have eaten enough, so eating more slowly around the table allows kids to notice 'I'm full'. At the table, only talk about positive things, make it a relaxed time, find out what has gone well in their lives, it's not a board meeting!*

4. *Don't get into 'bad food, good food'; call it 'everyday' food – the healthy things we eat all the time – and 'sometimes food' –*

which we have occasionally for a treat. Eating 'junk' food and feeling guilty about it just makes it worse. People binge then feel bad. Research shows that if you eat slowly and enjoy treat food, you actually don't eat as much of it.[14] If you are ashamed, you wolf it down.

5. *Be a family that moves. If dad and daughter walk the dog, or kick a ball around outside, or the whole family goes for a walk or to the park, a love of being physical will come naturally without it being 'exercise'.*

Everything here applies just as much to boys!

AN INDUSTRY OUT OF CONTROL

You may be shocked to learn that 95 per cent of obesity research is funded by the weight-loss industry.[15] No wonder our understanding of health and weight is so befuddled. The dieting industry is largely unregulated.

The food industry similarly requires tighter regulations. Why are toys sold with every Happy Meal, and high-sugar breakfast cereals marketed directly to children? If we want a healthier nation, environmental changes must take place, much like we saw with the tobacco industry losing its grasp as cigarettes were gradually banned from pubs, advertising outlawed, and cigarettes lost their glamorous packaging. Blaming and shaming the individual will never achieve population health.

Australia recently developed a National Advisory Board for Body Image which has taken up a voluntary code of conduct to get the beauty and fashion industries to adopt healthier approaches. Unfortunately the code was a flop. Chairperson of the advisory board Mia Freedman blogged 'NOTHING HAS CHANGED'. *Dolly Magazine* was awarded the government's 2012 body image awards (the centrepiece of the board's initiatives) despite resurrecting a modelling competition for 13-year-old girls. Sending the message that unless girls are hot, they're irrelevant, this was nothing short of an embarrassment. Other countries have begun making legislative changes. For example, Spain has looked into banning 'cult of the body' advertisements which promote plastic surgery and dieting products until 10 pm each night. In 2008 France made it illegal for anyone – including magazines and advertisers – to incite 'extreme thinness'. In 2012, the Israeli government introduced a law banning the use of underweight models in magazines and on the catwalk.

While some continue to blame parents for their child's poor body image, an open letter signed by 45 international health experts titled 'The Impact of Media Images on Body Image and Behaviours: A Summary of the Scientific Evidence' reported 'overwhelming evidence' that media images contributed to body dissatisfaction and disordered eating.[16] Another study reviewed 77 studies involving 15,000 participants which showed media images had greater impact on young people today than in the nineties.[17] In other words, despite all the body image initiatives, media images ultimately have more impact. Parents have some responsibility, though, and protective factors against disordered eating include helping children find physical activities they enjoy, modelling healthy behaviours, having regular family meals, eating breakfast every day, and fostering healthy self-esteem and body image. Governments must take a more aggressive approach to industry if we really want to see a healthy world for our girls.

WHAT ARE EATING DISORDERS?

Eating disorders are patterns of behaviour with food that are unhealthy or harmful if taken too far. Most people know of anorexia – a disorder within which people fail to eat enough food and run the risk of life-threatening weight loss. Thankfully death from this disorder is still relatively rare, but it is dangerous and anorexics need immediate help. Bulimia – vomiting up one's food after eating in order to limit or reduce weight, is much more common. In practice, eating disorders are blurred, and there are many people of normal weight, or above-average weight, who eat in a disordered way. In all cases, though, there is danger and a need to get professional help and advice early – the sooner it's addressed, the better chances of recovery.

Early Warning Signs

A parent should start to worry about a possible eating disorder if they notice a cluster of changes in their daughter, including:

- Weight fluctuations (whether the weight goes up or down);
- Change in mood, including becoming more anxious, angry, depressed or withdrawn;
- Increased preoccupation with body shape or weight, such as increased weighing or 'body checking';
- Changes in eating behaviour, such as eliminating food groups or specific meals; eating becoming more regimented or ritualistic; or 'regressed eating' – eating in a childlike way, for instance with special cups or child's crockery or cutlery;
- Increased distress around meal times or eating.

It is important to note that we are looking for a cluster of observable changes – any one of these behaviours alone could be due to another cause, such as an illness. Assessment and diagnosis of an eating disorder usually begins with checking there is no physical basis for the symptoms. It's only when multiple changes are observed together that an eating disorder may be considered to be the likely cause.

Disordered Thinking

Along with the changes to eating behaviour and mood, some unusual ways of thinking about food are evident in someone who is starting to have an eating disorder:

- Desire to maintain an unhealthily low body weight;
- An intense fear of weight gain or 'becoming fat';
- A distorted perception about their appearance;
- A preoccupation with food prospectively (worrying about forthcoming meals or meal planning) and retrospectively (experiencing intense guilt or shame about food consumed);
- False beliefs around food or weight loss/management (such as 'eating dinner after 6 pm will result in excessive weight gain'; or 'having four glasses of water before each meal will speed up the metabolism'.

The Actual Behaviours

Finally, the strongest clues to a disorder are actual eating behaviour. You may notice:

- Intentional restriction of food; for example eliminating meals like breakfast, eliminating entire food groups from the diet, or claims of a gluten or lactose or other new allergy.
- Binging, which is essentially consuming a large quantity of food in a short period of time, and eating with a sense of loss of control;
- Eating compulsively – feeling out of control while eating – or eating past fullness. (This can take place during normal meals and eating situations and can look relatively normal to a bystander, whereas binging is usually done in private and typically involves eating huge amounts of food.)
- Purging or 'getting rid of' food through unhealthy compensatory behaviours such as vomiting, abusing laxatives or excessive exercise.

The particular set of eating disorder behaviours exhibited will determine what diagnosis is made. It is normal for eating disorder behaviours to change over the course of the illness, and thus the diagnosis is also likely to change. In successful treatment a person with an eating disorder may swing to the opposite behaviour and their therapist will help them to manage and work through this.

What to Do

If you are concerned that your daughter might have an eating disorder, it is vital that you act immediately: early intervention is one of the best predictors of a complete recovery and you should never wait until your daughter is 'sick enough' to access help. Consult your family doctor or contact an eating disorder charity to arrange an assessment and find out the best way to access treatment in your area. Treatment for eating disorders is usually highly specialised and it is best to start with 'evidence-based treatment' – your GP or eating disorder charity will be able to advise on what this is in the case of your daughter.

The best predictor of success in treatment is the 'therapeutic alliance' – finding a good fit between the therapist, your daughter and yourself/your family. For individuals who don't respond to the first attempt of treatment, it is vital that further treatment be attempted. Ultimately recovery tends to take place with the match of the right therapist, the right approach and the right timing.

It is a good idea to read all you can about eating disorders, as this will assist you in being the best resource for your daughter's recovery.

It is very natural to feel worried, guilty or even angry at a person with an eating disorder. This can sometimes get in the way of being helpful. For example, some parents blame the person with the eating disorder for getting sick because of the impact the eating disorder has on their marriage or on the family. This resentment can make it difficult for parents to do what is required to support a sick daughter in her recovery – assisting her to access treatment or just being supportive and kind to her and listening to her feelings.

Five Myths About Eating Disorders

Myth 1: People choose to have an eating disorder.
Fact: Eating disorders are NOT a choice, they are serious psychological illnesses that develop over time and have complex psychological bases.

Myth 2: You must be thin to have an eating disorder.
Fact: Most people who experience eating disorders are in fact in the 'healthy weight range' or are even overweight.

Myth 3: Eating disorders only occur in females.
Fact: Eating disorders in males are rising, particularly in those aged under 14 years (a quarter of eating disorder diagnoses in that age group are now males). Males are also more likely to 'fly under the radar', given they are not expected to have eating disorders.

Myth 4: Anorexia is the only serious eating disorder.
Fact: Engagement in restricting food or weight loss practices such as vomiting or laxative abuse renders any person vulnerable to serious medical complications. Further, experiencing any eating disorder is distressing and isolating for sufferers and thus they are susceptible to a significant increased risk of self-harm and suicide.

Myth 5: People who develop eating disorders have been sexually abused.
Fact: Sexual abuse is a risk factor for developing many mental health conditions, including eating disorders. However, not everyone with eating disorders has been sexually abused.

Finally, if your daughter does develop an eating disorder you must remember that you are not to blame for the development of the illness, you are one of the best resources for her recovery. A comparable example is that a painkiller can help to remove a headache, but the headache is not caused by an absence of painkillers.

If your daughter does develop eating disorder symptoms, it is critical that you act on this immediately. Commencing treatment as soon as possible is vital as the illness can be avoided with early intervention; recovery outcomes will improve if treatment is commenced quickly. Ensure you learn as much as possible about eating disorders so you can be a resource in recovery. Hold the hope for your daughter because a complete and total recovery is possible for everyone.

SELF-HARM

Anyone involved with the lives of teenage girls today will encounter the problem of self-harm. It's become very common, and is an indicator of how much stress and anxiety kids are managing. It's important to realise and have in your understanding and response to your young person that this is an attempt by them to manage life (however odd this might seem) and that it serves a purpose for them. For them, it reduces stress. But at the same time, it's an indication that some help is definitely needed. You need to be calm, friendly and patient in talking to a teen who is harming herself.

This section has been adapted from the Lifeline Australia website which is compiled by a professional panel of mental health experts. You can read the whole site at https://www.lifeline.org.au/get-help/topics/self-harm. It's provided as a starting point and shouldn't replace the help of a qualified professional for your child's specific needs. Start by talking with your GP. They will help you to get the best professional care for your girl.

What Is Self-Harm?

Self-harm is usually defined as hurting oneself without wanting to die. It is a behaviour that is used to cope with difficult or painful feelings. Self-harm is relatively common. Research shows that about 1 per cent of people have self-harmed within the last month and about 8 per cent have done so in their lifetime. Most people start self-harming as a teenager or young adult. It can continue for many years and become a habit that is difficult to stop. Examples of self-harm may include:

- cutting the skin with sharp objects
- burning the skin
- hitting the body with fists or another object
- punching walls or other objects
- scratching or picking the skin, resulting in bleeding or welts
- pulling out hair.

Factors That May Increase Self-Harm Behaviour
The following are some factors associated with self-harm:

- a crisis or recent difficult life event (e.g. death of a loved one, relationship breakdown, difficulties at home or school, recent abuse or violence)
- depression, anxiety or another mental health issue
- misusing alcohol or drugs
- trauma or abuse during childhood
- physical illness or disability.

Reasons Why People Might Harm Themselves
People who self-harm find it difficult to talk about their feelings so they may use self-harm to express their emotions. They often hide their behaviour (e.g. wearing long sleeves, covering scars) and are not usually trying to gain attention or manipulate others.

Self-harm is usually not the same as a suicide attempt. However, self-harm may sometimes lead to a serious medical emergency. Also, people who self-harm are more likely to have had suicidal thoughts and over time may be at increased risk of dying by suicide. If life is in danger get help immediately.

It is important to get help for any mental health problems in order to help with the self-harm. Self-harm may be used to:

- deal with or stop negative emotions or pain, such as feeling sad, angry, upset, guilty or scared
- release tension or a build-up of emotions
- relieve feelings of loneliness or isolation
- punish themselves for something they've done, or something perceived as their fault
- feel 'alive' or 'real' or combat feelings of numbness
- feel more in control of their life
- communicate to people that they need some support when they feel unable to use words.

How to Help Someone Who Self-Harms

Supporting someone who self-harms can be tough. You may find it difficult to understand why they do it and find it upsetting or distressing. When you talk to the person, try to be calm, open and honest. Try not to be judgmental, shocked or take their behaviour personally. Try and see the situation from their point of view and understand why they engage in self-harm.

Let the person know that you support them and listen to them express their feelings.

Encourage the person to get support from health professionals like their GP or mental health professional and offer to go with them to their appointments if they are scared or uncomfortable.

Don't forget to look after yourself. Helping someone who self-harms can be draining and upsetting, so get support and look after your physical and emotional needs too.

In a Nutshell

- Both under-eating and over-eating are growing problems for girls worldwide.
- Dieting is actually not helpful in losing weight, and in fact often makes the problem worse.
- 'Fat-shaming' is a cruel and unhelpful trend in our culture, yet some schools, government programmes and TV programmes encourage it.
- Eating with awareness and focusing on health, not weight, are the best strategies.
- Eating disorders like anorexia and bulimia (which is far more common) are mental illnesses, not choices made freely. They involve disordered thinking as well as eating in extreme ways. Noticing the early warning signs and getting help are the best things you can do.
- Know the warning signs of self-harm, and raise it without drama or blame. And do get help.

Chapter 11

Alcohol and Other Drugs

Paul Dillon lives in the inner city. He can tell you about the street price of amphetamines, and what quality ice is coming into the country right now. He knows what to do if someone has overdosed or drunk themselves into a coma. Paul is Australia's best-known drug educator, and has been for years, working with schools and groups all over the country to make sure kids have a clear perspective and can keep themselves and their friends from dying in the name of a good time.[1]

Indeed, Paul may well be responsible for the fact that since 2002 drug use and drinking among young people have actually gone down. He has some surprising insights and methods to help parents know when to relax and when to wake up, in guiding their kids and themselves in a world of mind-altering chemicals, legal and illegal. When Paul visits a school, he shows some interesting slides. Most people are familiar with the graphs showing lots of kids using alcohol, less smoking, quite a few using cannabis, and so on down the list to ecstasy and heroin, but Paul simply turns this upside down. Depending a little on the country in which you are reading this, but pretty much consistently across the Western world, we have the following picture:

- *Although many 17-year-olds have drunk alcohol, most do not drink to excess regularly, with some rarely touching the stuff. Over 25 per cent of this age range say they are 'non-drinkers' and almost 10 per cent have never drunk alcohol at all.*
- *More than 70 per cent of 17-year-old secondary school students* have never smoked cannabis and probably won't.
- *97 per cent of secondary school students* have never used hallucinogens.

- *96 per cent* have never used amphetamines, *and even of the 4 per cent who have, most only tried them once or twice in the last year.*
- *Ditto for heroin or morphine.*
- *Cocaine is the same: 98 per cent never use it and the two per cent only used it once or twice.*
- *Ecstasy is a bit worse – only 92 per cent have never used it (!) and of those who do most are quite occasional users.*

Paul gazes across the sea of young people sitting in school assembly halls and multi-purpose rooms to watch his presentation, and when these slides come up he sees dozens of young people sit a little taller. *They are the non-drinking, non-drugging kids suddenly realising they are in the majority.* This is really important for them, and you, to know about. Suddenly all that panic about kids getting wasted, and the pressure that this *is what you are supposed to do to be cool*, starts to fade away.

In fact, not only are most kids of school age quite happy to avoid drugs and drinking but (apart from a slight rise in the use of ecstasy) their usage has been falling, slowly but steadily, all through the 2000s. Today's young people are a bit over all that.

That's the good news, especially on drugs. In particular Paul is at great pains to point out that drugs are a very minor problem for a small number of young people (for whom, of course, they are a big problem indeed). But he is not at all soft on harm reduction, alcohol, he says, is a different matter.

Alcohol products, which are legally produced and sold, and heavily promoted (in fact carefully designed) to appeal to young women, are destroying brains and causing huge risks to safety from accidents and violence. I've heard Paul come close to suggesting (and I am inclined to agree) that the alcohol industry probably encourages paranoia about drugs so that parents will be relatively relaxed that their daughters only use alcohol. More on the alcohol industry later.

For years the folklore about alcohol is that a little bit won't hurt you, and that the 'Mediterranean approach' of letting kids sip a little wine at mealtimes helps to make them sensible drinkers and takes away the 'rebellion' in drinking. A book by a leading girls' schools organisation actually advised this just last year.

It's a nice theory, but it's recently been proven totally wrong. Having small amounts of alcohol in childhood or the early to mid-teens is now known to change the brain in startling ways, making it more vulnerable to alcohol, and alcoholism, afterwards. Kids shouldn't be allowed anywhere near it.

In fact, the brain effects of even modest amounts of drinking support the strong argument for adopting the US age limit of 21, which works fine for them. The fake licence issues tend to take place at around the age of 19 in the US, whereas for us it's more like 16. That's three or four years of better brain protection.

And although Paul's upside-down graphs make a good point, for alcohol the usage is still concerning, even in a minority group. Around one in 17 young people drink at dangerous levels every week. For women (whose bodies are smaller and have a different chemistry) the level of dangerous drinking is consuming more than four standard drinks in one episode, while for girls who don't yet have a developed liver (which doesn't happen until around the age of 21!) it should be much less than that. Six per cent of girls who are still at school drink at levels that are dangerous for fully grown women at least once a week.

The newest concern, which few parents or girls have yet absorbed, is that alcohol is a risk factor for breast cancer, accounting for about a third of all breast cancers. (While breast cancer has a genetic component, it is almost always caused by environmental toxins of some kind or other. Flooding your bloodstream with ethanol is not good for soft tissues.)

This, then, is the picture that we described in our mental health overview earlier. Most girls are fine, but the group that are not fine are in real trouble.

So far we've been looking at kids still at school. One of the wonderful things about school is that it has a huge, protective, mental-health benefit. For most kids, schools are still friendly places with routine and structure, where there are adults who care about you, and friends on tap with a wide range of ideas and attitudes.

When kids leave school, all the mental health indicators – suicide rates, self-harm, drinking and drugs, depression and anxiety – leap upwards. It's lonely out in the big world.

What Parents of Girls Should Know and Teach

The use of drugs by girls is not correlated to any of the things you might think. It's not connected to income – rich girls and poor girls are at equal risk. It's not related to educational level. It's not connected to intelligence or ability. Only one factor stands out as a reliable predictor: *parental supervision or monitoring.* Parents who know where you are, know what you are doing, and are around and in your life, tend not to have kids who drink or use drugs. And if things do occasionally go haywire, they care and they get involved to make sure it doesn't happen again.

This involvement isn't 'guard the door' suspicion, but caring conversations, firmness around where you are and with whom, and friendly but clear negotiations about proving you are able to stay safe and careful.

All the adolescent experts I spoke to in writing this book were very critical (that's the polite word) of a certain kind of parent who wants to be their child's friend – the mum who buys the drinks, the dad who gives his daughter £50 when she heads into the city to 'party' with her friends. (Party used to be a word for friends who loved each other hosting everyone at their home for delicious food, drinks, conversation and dancing, now it just means getting smashed. It's done in anonymous clubs and bars where you can't hear yourself speak. That's intentional – if kids start talking, they don't drink as much. The owners want them hot, restless and revved, because that sells more drinks.)

Around 35 per cent of all the alcohol drunk by kids of school age (and therefore illegal drinkers) is provided by parents.[2] But then, at least it's not drugs!

One particular drug is almost exclusively the choice at 'parties' (i.e. clubs) and that is ecstasy. Ecstasy makes you feel energetic and loving, it releases a week's supply of endorphins from your body (which is why you feel crap for a week afterwards). The problem is that it's usually made in a bikie warehouse by someone called Slug who doesn't always know, or care, what goes into it. Nobody knows what they are taking. This is the thing to quietly, and calmly, explain to your teenager. This stuff doesn't come from Switzerland.

It's possible we are making our kids too trusting of pills overall. We prescribe them to an awful lot of little boys who just need more chance to run around. And when a child has a headache, we reach for the Panadol. Paul points out that 90 per cent of adolescent headaches are caused by dehydration, and a nice glass of water might be more help.

The Alcohol Pushers[3]

Several years ago the alcohol industry was worried because drinking levels were steady or falling. Their best customers had died young. The companies needed a new market, because in industry, growth is every-

thing. Their researchers talked to teenage girls. (In the US they pay schools $500 and get access to schoolkids for all kinds of research into how better to harm them.) It turned out that girls don't like the taste of spirits. This was a tragic waste of a good market, and so the industry devised alcopops – fizzy and sugary drinks that tasted like juice but were loaded with rum, brandy, vodka or gin. And, whoopee, girls began to drink them by the caseload.

In Australia the government, under pressure from

health groups, attempted to raise the tax on these drinks. The industry created a storm, and a compromise was reached (lobbyists don't just vote, like the rest of us, they exert other forms of influence). Alcopop consumption fell, though not enough. Girls also got used to spirits. Today, to pre-empt the cost of drinks in clubs, you can see girls on trains into the city slugging supermarket liquor so they can arrive pre-smashed.

Wherever you are reading this, you can test your politicians' integrity. Ask them to tax alcohol heavily, especially those products favoured by young people or designed to entice them. Young drinkers are very price-sensitive, a 20 per cent price rise often deals them out. Get them to ban all advertising of alcohol aimed at the young – it can survive as an honest industry providing a valuable product, it just won't be a cash cow that costs us all in hospitals and road crashes. Demand that they raise the drinking age to 21, when it will do the least brain damage to still-growing brains, and gives a couple more years of maturity and life experience to deal with its effects. If they don't, individually or as a party, support these changes, then you know who owns them, and it's not the voters.

Binge Drinking

So despite the good news of the big picture, a small but sizeable cohort of girls and young women are drinking enough for the rest of us. These girls drink so much, one or more nights a week, that their bodies are permanently being changed. Teenagers do not have fully grown kidneys; they cannot absorb or process the alcohol from their bloodstreams anywhere near as fast. Serious harm occurs to their growing brain and they are 60 per cent more likely to have an alcohol problem as an adult.

Binge drinking by girls and young women has swept the world, even reaching countries where alcohol hasn't been a problem in the past – such as France or Italy. The boys can't believe their luck; the sexual availability of these girls has soared. They just don't seem to care.

The reason for the upswing in girls drinking at dangerous levels is a combination of factors. Venues for entertainment and socialising are heavily alcohol-focused. There is a massive marketing effort to make drinking look adult and cool. The pressure to conform and just drink to fit in is enormous. But there seems to be something else, too, a kind of desperate wish to get wasted, a kind of temporary suicide, to knock reality out with an almost self-destructive zeal. All the pressures we have listed through this book add up, and for some girls it comes out in drinking, for others in cutting, others in disordered eating, others in random sex. Sometimes, it's all of the above. These girls need help.

What to Do?

If you are a parent, love your daughter. Do all the things in this book from the time she is small. If she starts problem drinking anyway, get help. Alcoholism is a metabolic condition in some people and just has to be managed.

Don't give drinks to underage kids. Don't drink more than the odd glass yourself if you don't need to, or only on special occasions and moderately. Especially try not to drink when you are stressed, so that she sees you 'needing' alcohol or, worse, affected by it. That's role-modelling of the worst kind.

Don't let her simply go out into the city to cruise clubs until she is old enough to take care of herself. Depending on where you live, that could be 21. Have a definite deal about getting home, and a rescue arrangement that you will go get her ANYWHERE ANYTIME when needed.

The aim is for your daughter to be able to go out, have a good time, and not be harmed. You are on the same side as her, just more aware of the big picture. While she is under 18, her life is your responsibility. But even when she is older, and still living under your roof, you have an opportunity to intervene, in a friendly and concerned way, to keep her safe. Even a caring flatmate would do that. Being home at an agreed time and not coming back drunk are reasonable requirements in any household where people care about each other.

Esther's Law

Esther, who helps manage my teacher seminars, is barely 25, and a warm and idealistic member of generation Y. I asked her how her friends dealt with partying. Simple, she said, we have the Voice of Reason. She and her friends realised they needed someone, rather like the designated driver, who stayed straight and could decide whether it was time to go home, if that street was a good place to walk, and any other decisions about people and places that would keep them out of harm. Each night they went out together, in a group of five or six, they would vote for who would be the Voice of Reason. That person would only have one drink. And the pact was – what she says, we all do, without even a moan of complaint.

I asked whether this was an onerous task, suspecting for some reason that it might fall to her more often than not? Oh no, she assured me, it's kind of an honour. Some of the girls we would never choose. We do rotate it a little, but three or four of us kind of take it seriously that we love each other and we get everyone home safe. We're proud of it.

Chapter 12

Mirror, Mirror on the Screen

What to Do About Social Media

Every one of us has an idea of who we are. When we are little, this mostly comes from the people around us. Parents tell us we are kind, or funny, or smart, a teacher or coach at school encourages us for not giving up, for putting in a good effort. Our friends – or other less friendly kids – chastise us or encourage us.

Gradually young people grow stronger in their own sense of self. But even as adults, it's still a fragile thing – if we spend time in a strange city, or just out and about and nobody acknowledges us, we start to feel less of a person. A warm smile or a friend greeting us at the shopping centre can lift our spirits. Research[1] shows that this connection is not just a luxury or a feel-good thing – it's the key to mental health and even makes us live longer.

As we get older, we build our 'tribe' – the support network who know us and value us. Teenagers do this intently as they are shaping their identities, but with the growth of the internet, their tribe has become a very strange one indeed. The problem didn't begin with social media though – kids were already in a bad place before that. For thousands of years girls had grown up around aunties, uncles and grandparents and even 50 years ago, they spent four or five times as much time with older adults than they do now. School is a very unnatural grouping of same-age kids, with just one adult to 30 kids, and very little personal conversation or being noticed. So adolescence was already an isolating and insecure experience, because we took adults away from kids and left them with their peer group. Instagram and Snapchat arrived when kids were already full of self-doubt and loneliness. It offered connection – friends! Praise! Instant feedback! And of course, it was a false promise.

Suddenly a whole load of strangers were commenting and approving or disapproving or gaslighting or grooming them. They looked for approval from people who didn't give a damn, or worse, got their kicks from being incredibly mean. Even real-life friends, rendered distant and blunt through not being in the room, turned nasty and insensitive. Or tried to be supportive, but were not actually there to give a hug or dry a tear or provoke a laugh.

Social media researcher Toni Hassan uses the analogy of a mirror.[2] For thousands of years there were no mirrors! We barely even saw our own reflection, except perhaps in a still pool. Anyone could assume they were good-looking. Then mirrors were invented and self-consciousness was born. Who today doesn't check the mirror, not just for crumbs in their eyebrows but to check 'who I am today'?

Today, though, the screen is our mirror. And it silently screams at you, 'you are nobody'. It's a horrible place. I am not exaggerating here. Go on the internet and say anything different or vulnerable about yourself – for example that you are LGBTI – and within a few minutes someone will tell you to kill yourself.

Girls use social media about 50 per cent more than boys do.[3] They take elaborate selfies, study them, take a few dozen more, change their make-up, hoist their cleavage and click again. Then they post it and wait for the reflection. We adults are little better – we post our family holiday photos, what we're having for lunch or news articles we like and then wait for the response. It can be harmless and connecting if you have a robust self-esteem. But for an insecure young person seeking an identity (which means not having a well-developed one on the inside yet), this can be crushing.

The Links Are Clear

For a few years nobody was sure if social media was fine or a problem. But that doubt was swept away by some very clear findings. Professor Jill Twenge's blockbuster research released in 2017[4,5] reported that a sudden and alarming growth in teen suicide (which had previously been falling) exactly matched the years when ownership of smartphones began to surge among young people. This generation of kids had replaced real connection with online connection.

Twenge's studies were carefully controlled and used large datasets. They were also very balanced. She found many positives in the new trend for kids to meet online instead of getting together in shopping malls or cars. Girls in Twenge's 'iGen' generation are having sex later (on average a year later), drinking less, getting pregnant less! But they are lonelier. They aren't going out skating or surfing, visiting friends, playing sport, or talking to mum or grandma or dad or their kid sister. Their friendship network is very intense, but it is less personal. It's made up of likes and snippets of text and tweets. And somehow that isn't nourishing. It doesn't send your endorphins singing or your shoulder muscles relaxing or your heart easing in anything like the same way. You don't have really close or deep conversations.

Twenge found that there was a direct connection with the amount of time spent on screen and feeling unhappy. And a whole generation were less happy. Suicide among 12–14-year-old girls (her studies were in the US) trebled between 2007 and 2015. Trebled. That's about as significant as a statistic can get.[6]

What Goes Wrong?

How exactly might social media cause suicide? Twenge believes the main suspect is the bullying that happens online, quite routinely, among teen girls, leading them to feel increasingly left out (almost 50 per cent report feeling excluded at times). But there are other factors too. For example, we know that the blue light emitted from screens triggers alertness in the brain and keeps kids awake and restless. And lack of sleep increases depression. (Some phone manufacturers now install blue light filters to reduce the effect.) Sleep experts strongly advise that kids or adults not use any screens for at least an hour before going to bed.

What to Do

Two things. Wait longer to give them devices. And put some time limits around when they can use them. Kids of primary age or mid-high school age probably don't even need smartphones at all. A dumb phone (that only makes calls) is enough for safety and arrangements. Why give them expensive equipment that only makes them miserable and stressed? But don't take my word for any of this. Here (don't laugh) is a transcript of a Facebook discussion that I hosted on this very thing.

We have 70,000 parents of girls from many nations around the world on the *Raising Girls* Facebook page. And what they told me was very helpful. In fact, rather revolutionary.

Josie (Cork, Ireland): We've been trying this thing, as a family. We all put our devices on the charger at teatime, before we sit down to eat. And we leave them there until the next morning. Nobody uses their iPads or phones or laptops after the evening meal. Kids or adults.

Me: You're kidding? You can do that? LOL

Josie: Yes, it's working fine. It was a bit of a shock. We just thought, if we expect the kids to do it, we ought to do it as well. It's changing things at home, we talk more, the kids find games to play with each other instead of in their rooms.

Maree (Brisbane, Australia): A few of our friends are doing that too, and we started about a month ago.

Me: Hi Maree, how is it affecting your daughter/s?

Maree: That's the thing. Our daughter was the reason we did it, she was just always online during the night, checking her social media, she was tired in the mornings, and ratty and stressed, with rings under her eyes.

Me: How old is she?

Maree: She's 13. And now, well, she's a different girl. She sleeps well. She wakes up happy and keen to go to school, whereas before she dreaded it. She is a lot nicer to live with. And we talk more.

Josie: Same here, that's the big difference we noticed. Both our girls – they are 13 and 16 – are happier now. The change was almost instantaneous. We brought in the 'no devices after dinner' rule, which was hard for us as parents as we used to often be on screens ourselves, especially my husband. But our kids, especially the older one, just started to chill out more, and not be so fretful. I think the schoolyard politics and friendship angst was just keeping her awake at night. It didn't have any upside for her, but she felt she had to 'keep up'. In reality, she didn't miss anything worth missing, and was better off out of it until the next day, when most of it had died down or moved on. I think her being a calmer person helped her friends too. Several of our friends' families have brought in the same rule.

The discussion went on along these lines for a while, and then something happened that has never happened before on my Facebook page. An actual teenager made an appearance.

Laurel: Hello, I am 15, I hope you don't mind me commenting here, I know this is a parents' page. I just wanted to say, my mum and dad brought in that rule. And I am really grateful that they did. I could never have given up social media during the night on my own, even though I knew it was stressing me out. It's just too hard to give up. Having the rule and everyone's phones and iPads on the charger in the kitchen, you just get used to it. After a few nights, it feels normal. I am glad my mum and dad brought in this rule. I could blame them – haha!

So that's what's happening, and perhaps it's worth thinking about at your place too. And how very like teens, who with their still forming brains do need us to do our job and have a few fences around their mental health, which they find hard to provide themselves. And they're honest enough to know that!

In a Nutshell

- We all need a 'tribe' to support our wellbeing, especially children and young people.
- Today, kids may seek their tribe among strangers on social media instead of face to face with people who care about them.
- Researchers found that suicide suddenly began to rise when social media useage grew.
- Many parents don't give their kids smartphones too young and limit using devices in bedrooms and after dinner, and are finding their kids are happier as a result.

Part Three

Girls and
Their Parents

Chapter 13

Girls and Their Mums

There's one fact about raising a girl that nobody disagrees with, and that is the centrality of mothers. The reason for this is simple: a mother is the role model, the person of the same gender who has the most effect, from the earliest time, for 95 per cent of girls. A stay-at-home dad could be the main caregiver and have a huge effect; a substitute aunty or grandmother might step in for a mum who can't be there, but for most girls, Mum is the person who teaches them what it means to be a woman. That's an awesome thing.

A girl might at different times adore her mum or hate her, admire her or criticise her – usually, in the 20 years of growing up, they will do all of the above! But however it goes, no daughter ever says her mother wasn't hugely important. Long after you are gone, your daughter will remember your smile and your touch, what you taught her, and how you made her feel. She will pass all this on in the way she loves her children, and that love will go on down the generations.

How Role-Modelling Works

When you think about it, what children have to learn while growing up is incredibly complex. It's not just things like riding a bike or ballet – everything we do has to be learnt. How to be patient, how to give orders, how to argue with a husband amicably so he really gets what you are saying, how to use humour to keep spirits up when exhausted, how to love – these are not things you can learn from books. We learn to be human from watching other humans. Without role models, we would be clueless, and our lives impossibly hard. People without good role models often end up in trouble or in jail. (Support workers for 'mothers at risk' often find that they have simply never seen someone

discipline a child kindly, only pinch them, lock them in a cupboard, or slap them on the face. They literally did not know there was another way.)

The brains of children are wired to watch and copy. Special networks of nerves called 'mirror neurons' link our eyes and our muscles, so we observe what others do and take that into our own behaviour without even knowing it. You will notice you have mannerisms that your mother or father had. That's your mirror neurons at work. This is why each child becomes like the people they grow up around. Musicians create musicians, gardeners or animal lovers create a new generation of the same. If your kids love you, they will want to be like you.

So, brace yourself – you know where this is going, don't you? Your daughter is going to turn into you. Plus whatever other role models or extra ingredients she can add to improve on the basic model! She will carry you inside her. If you can be your best self as a mother, then she will get the best start – she will take in the very best you have to give.

BEING A STEPMUM

One-third of all mums today are stepmums.[1] Stepmothering a daughter is a generous and beautiful act, because the love and closeness has to grow from scratch. Stepmothers tell me that the secret is in not forcing oneself on a daughter who didn't choose you, and may have powerful feelings of both loyalty and loss towards her biological mum. Don't aim to replace her, but to grow a new relationship alongside her. Trust and intimacy take time – stepchildren have to come to you, on an emotional level. Be calm, be kind, and love will grow.

Throughout history, millions of kids have found additional or different mothers from the ones they were born to. Nobody needs to get less. A girl needs lots of love, and the more role models in her life, the better off she is.

Cleaning Up Your Act

So let's get practical. What are the ways in which your role-modelling might lead her to get a good or a bad start? Cast a quick glance over your life ...

- *Are you able to get along with men, or is that a disaster area in your life?*
- *Do you know how to make and keep good friends?*
- *Do you know how to relax?*
- *Do you know how to keep your promises?*
- *Do you know how to keep going when the road is hard and long?*

She can learn these things from you.

There are other, more everyday things we show our daughters inadvertently. Stress is a big one. In my talk called 'Secrets of Happy Children', I tell parents a rather stunning thing. Your children cannot be more relaxed than you. That's because, at least in the early years, their level of stress rises and falls on the levels of their mum's and dad's and anyone else nearby. They are like a cork bobbing about on the waves of their mum and dad's stress levels. Even newborn babies know about this. I once worked with a family in therapy who brought their baby along in a bassinet. The baby would vomit every time they got to a certain difficult topic. The rest of the hour, it was peaceful – but very alert!

Stress may seem difficult to control, but with help you can learn how to calm your body even in tough situations. Pregnancy is a great time to start a yoga relaxation or a meditation class. It's easiest to learn from someone you like (your mirror neurons will help you). A tape or DVD is next best (a book is helpful, but you will have to really be determined).

Every day you can choose how stressful you want your life to be, and what your daughter will observe and learn from you. The way you drive is a classic example. If you yell at other drivers, curse them for going slowly, drive up close behind them, make racist comments or even just tap your fingers anxiously on the wheel, your daughter sees that. Sometimes we have no idea how dangerous our children perceive our driving to be. My daughter told her mum that she didn't want to drive with me. My driving style is not fast, it's actually way too relaxed. I leave it to the last minute to change lanes, do creative u-turns and depend on my amazing ability to back into parking spots. It was scaring her witless. I had to develop a whole new approach to driving, because I really wanted her to feel safe with me.

Girls watch their mums (and dads) for the way they treat other people – if they are kind to others, if they volunteer for things, belong to community groups, stop and help someone who looks lost or distressed in the high street ...

Having kids means keeping a check on our emotions. They are often really frightened by unexplained intensity. We need to moderate ourselves, because they are little and vulnerable, something we easily forget. We can have and show our feelings, but not be overwhelmed by them.

Each gender has risk factors – in boys it can be arrogance. With daughters, though, we have to guard against setting an example of martyrdom. A martyr is someone who doesn't put their own needs into the equation. Our girls need to see us taking a healthy interest in our own activities, our own health, our own creative time, our own spirit. Otherwise, how will they ever learn to do the same?

Maximising Your Example

You can magnify your role-modelling in one simple way: by explaining why you do things. Girls listen to what we say, even before they can speak. By explaining our choices and actions, they get a mental map of why people act the way they do. People who act badly often do so because they are not thinking much, they simply react emotionally to everything that comes along. People who act well have usually figured out some guidelines for living, and that helps them choose. So share your reasons with your daughter; one example might be striving to understand others' motives: 'That person is speeding, but perhaps it's an emergency, or they are having a bad day. Hope they'll be okay.'

An important thing to teach your kids is that there is long term and short term. Finishing your schoolwork is hard when you would rather be swimming or playing computer games, but it's better to finish it so you can really relax. By secondary school, the idea can be absorbed that if you want a job that is fun, pays well, and where other people don't boss you around, you need some qualifications. So it's worth putting in a bit of effort and passing Years 10, 11 and 12. And so on.

Explain your values to your kids: that it's good to take care of yourself, but also to be caring for others, that it really helps if people keep their agreements, that most situations can be solved with some compromise, that everyone's voice counts, that honesty is better in the long run. They might roll their eyes, but you will see them adopting your philosophy a day or two later, or with their friends when you aren't even around.

So ask yourself, what are the core beliefs that you live your life by? Be sure to let your daughter know.

Letting Go

If all goes well, mothers and daughters end up being lifelong friends. However, in the late teen years, some distance is necessary if they are to grow and become themselves. Also, they need to have other role models in their life. Recognising this means we can avoid clinging to them and taking this distancing personally. It can be hard, but our kids do need space. Micky Foss, a mother in northern New South Wales, told me this story.

My best friend's 17-year-old daughter stays with us overnight once a week.

The other morning when she left for school, I went with her to the front door, helped her with some of her things, kissed her goodbye and wished her a good day. She said, in a jubilant and excited voice: 'Oh, you are so sweet! You take me to the door, help me and kiss me goodbye. My mother would never do that. She just calls "Bye" from inside the house, and then I leave. I wish she would kiss me goodbye.'

I went inside and mused over that for a while. The fact of the matter is that my friend's daughter is my 'substitute' daughter. I would love to accompany my own 16-year-old girl to the door, kiss her goodbye, and with all my heart wish her a good day. However, she would hate that.

I surmised from this that, no matter what mothers do with their teenage daughters, the daughters appear to want the opposite – i.e. whatever they don't get or have.

Why? From how I see it, this is part of the natural separation process. My daughter would think I was 'babying' her: she would think I thought her incapable of getting herself out the door, and she would not want my kisses. I used to do all that, and she used to lap it up. Not any more! She has to develop and form herself as an individual without her mother (me) doing what I did when she was little. And although I have known my friend's daughter since she was a baby, I am not her mother, so she has no need or desire to separate from me. She can, without any emotional dilemmas, enjoy my care and love for her.

I told my friend how her daughter responded to me. My friend will now take her daughter to the door in the morning and kiss her goodbye. My bet is that, within a week, her daughter will push her away and say: 'Leave me be! How old do you think I am?'

Time will tell ...

Home as a Haven

Something I have learnt from great parents is worth passing on. It's good to look at the whole 'vibe' in your house – the emotional atmosphere that you as parents create for everyone to live in.

The big world outside is stressful. Schools are often way too big and anonymous; the school day is hurried, nerves get jangled and frayed. Often our towns are grimy and strangers who don't care much about us are all around. Some kids even have to deal with hostility or violence. There is very little natural space in our lives to be quiet with nature, the wind and sky or water. Because of all this, the need for home to be peaceful and safe is essential – especially for girls, whose senses are fine-tuned to the nuances of sensory inputs all around them.

So it really helps that home is a calm place. It doesn't mean that you don't have some fun TV on straight after school for half an hour to chill out, or some music, but notice the 'temperature' – is it peaceful, or jangling? Do you welcome the children home, give them some food and drink and encourage them to unwind, or pile on some demands and rush about yourself?

Routine and structure soothes children, they know what is what, and can be more free and creative because they don't have to be hypervigilant.

Here are some other things that help:

- *Shared meals at fixed times, where everyone sits at a table and there is no TV, really helps (there is even research to show this).*[2]
- *Set bedtimes and set times to get ready for bed, and for activities that lead to bedtime – like baths or showers, story reading, or reading time for leisure before they fall asleep.*

- *An electronic blackout around bedtime; phones should be left on their chargers in the kitchen, not under the pillow to bother them with playground politics late into the night.*
- *Seasonal rituals that are exciting, with an enlarged family circle and the buzz of being in a large group where they still belong and matter.*
- *Silly games like Pictionary or family concerts and talent quests among the extended family to help people be playful across all generations.*
- *Great celebrations of birthdays – not expensive, but with time and effort and some care to make it something the kids really remember.*
- *One-to-one time, with just Mum, or just Dad, and daughter, such as a weekend away once a term, just the two of you, where you sleep, cook, do activities and talk with nobody else – no partner, no other siblings – so she can actually feel your 100 per cent care for her and store this in her memory banks.*
- *Visits and sleepovers with favourite aunts or grandparents, again to have that one-to-one opportunity.*
- *Family holidays where everyone can chill out – avoid expensive resorts where some bored young adults run 'Kidz Clubs' and parents don't get any closer to their children than they do during the rest of the year. Often holidays are the times children remember as the most special in their lives, because they saw their parents actually relaxed and happy and glad to be with them.*
- *An annual clean-up of unwanted clothes, books and toys, perhaps at the start of the new school year, to make their rooms spacious, clean and 'new' – and to give stuff to where it can help someone else.*

This has been a broad sweep of ideas, and I hope some of them have captured your imagination.

Motherhood carries some natural grief: your children are headed out into the big world, and the better you raise them, the further they may go. But, despite the distance, kids raised with love grow closer and closer to their mothers. Your place in their hearts will always be as if you were standing right beside them.

A GREAT FILM ABOUT MOTHERS

You might have heard of a movie called *Spanglish*, with Adam Sandler and Paz Vega in the lead roles. Often mistaken for a comedy and overlooked, this wonderful film about a Mexican mother and daughter coming to live with a wealthy American family tells a powerful story about mothering girls. The values of the two cultures are sharply in contrast: in one, possessions, fashion and shopping are how love is shown, and this puts deep-down pressure on everyone. In the other, loyalty, effort and being true to yourself are what matters most.

In the opening sequences, the American mother buys her daughter clothes one size too small to 'motivate' her to lose weight. The daughter's excitement at seeing the clothes turns to bitter disappointment, and the scene is set for some real learning.

The Mexican daughter and the American daughter are touching to watch as they struggle with growing up. The contrast between how daughters are raised in each culture is very enlightening. The movie ends with an unforgettable quote from the Mexican daughter, some years later as she looks back on her childhood. She is writing an application for a college scholarship, which asks about 'who she is': 'If I get accepted to this college I will be thrilled, but it won't define me. My sense of who I am comes powerfully and happily from one single fact – that I am my mother's daughter.'

Imagine if your daughter is able to say that when she is a woman, grown-up, independent and strong. What would it take, for that to be so? Wouldn't that be worth a whole lot of time and care? Wouldn't that just be amazing?

In a Nutshell

- For better or worse, mums are the most powerful influence in a girl's life. This is because you role-model a very strong example of how to be a female human being.
- Just knowing this can cause you to re-examine a lot of the things you do.
- Especially important is how you role-model relating to others – including her father. How you drive a car, how you speak about others – everything you do becomes part of her.
- A big issue is the stress level you create in the home and in your life. You can literally set the stress levels in your daughter's body by how you set your own.
- Letting go is part of helping her grow up. From the age of 16, she may at times want you not to crowd her too much. This doesn't mean you don't stay in charge, though.
- Get it right with your daughter, get to know her at a deep level, and it will be a life-long joy to you both.

Chapter 14
Girls and Their Dads

They pause at the top of the stairs, the father and his little girl. She peers down the long flight of steps, and frowns a little. Then, without even looking beside her, she reaches for his hand, and it's there, and she grasps it. Now she steps out boldly down the first step, and the second, as he does the same beside her. She is singing to herself in rhythm as they descend. And he feels pretty good too.

Fathers, to their young daughters, seem to be almost magical beings. They often go away to strange places and back each day. Their voices are booming, deep and loud. They smell funny, but mostly in a good way. Often they represent fun, excitement, and a stirring up of the daily routine. All being well, they make Mummy smile. Girls of all ages deeply want to love their dads and be loved back by them.

In recent decades, we've woken up to the value and importance of dads. (As late as the 1970s, if a mother died and there was no other family, the children would automatically have been put in an orphanage, the father would not have even been given the chance to try and raise them. How shattering that double grief must have been to thousands of dads and their children.)

Today we know that dads feel as deeply, can care as well, and are as vitally important as mums. (And a mum and dad who work as a team are pure gold.) Girls with an involved dad have been found in many studies to have higher self-esteem, get better school marks, and are less likely to become pregnant early, or have problems with alcohol or drugs. Dads are good for you.

As this message has spread in recent years, dads are stepping up. Today's young fathers spend *three times as long* with their children each day: talking, playing and teaching them, than the fathers of a generation ago.[1] That's a huge change.

Here are the main ways in which a father is important to a girl ...

He's Strong and Safe

Very early on a small child decides whether Dad is one of two things: a source of safety and protection, or a source of danger and threat. Safety and trust are the most central feelings daughters enjoy with a good, kind dad. We need to be reminded, we grown-ups, that we are like giants to our small children, towering in the sky. I have come to think that a father should make a pledge to himself and, silently, to his small children: 'I will never hit or hurt you. I will strive never ever to frighten you.' Every child should be able to say 'I always feel safe with my dad.'

This can be as simple as using a softer voice. *Girls' hearing is more acute than that of boys.* They often think you are shouting when you think you are just using a firm voice. (When our kids were small, my partner Shaaron would point out to me that my voice was far louder than I realised. I was embarrassing to take to the supermarket! But worse, I could sound scary when I thought I was just being, well, *emphatic.* This was not the kind of father that I wanted to be.)

Our physical strength has to be used for good. This strength, rather like a powerful horse or dog, has a wonderful appeal to a small girl. Dads who get down on the floor and play with their daughters, being a horse for them to ride or a monster that they can wrestle and defeat, with much struggle and noise, give them a sense of safety and also create daughters *with a higher capacity for excitement.* It's as if they borrow our power and make it part of them.

This early investment of fun time leads to a daughter who wants to have adventures and share activities with us all through her growing up. There is something about seeing a girl fishing with her dad, or surfing, or out walking with him on a windy Sunday afternoon, that touches the heart and bodes well for her life.

He Stays Connected

Most new dads experience a rush of amazement, responsibility and protective care when their little girl is born. The question, though, is, 'Will he stay engaged?' In the past, confused about their role, or awkward about taking it up, just too busy, or worst of all not interested, many twentieth-century dads failed the test. *Their daughters carried this as a deep wound.* Misbehaviour in the teenage years, rude and rebellious acting out and, worst of all, trashing themselves with careless boys, booze, drugs and cars, was the way daughters took revenge.

Not being loved by a dad can make a girl not love herself. Mums can compensate for this, but not completely. This was the tragedy of the industrial era, when dads worked long hours and came home exhausted. Just as for the mother when a marriage breaks down, the children often blame themselves for a breakdown in their relationship with their dad; daughters conclude that 'If dad is too busy to have time for me, it must be that I am boring and not worth it.'

When I talk about fathers to audiences of parents, there is always a point where I see women around the auditorium quietly shedding a tear as they listen. Some are grieving for what they *didn't* get, and some are remembering the love they *did* receive. It's an intense and life-changing relationship, a dad and his daughter.

TRAGICALLY IGNORED

A friend of mine goes out with his teenage daughter most Saturday mornings. They sit down and have a talk, because a lot of the week he is busy and comes home late. One day they see a girl she knows from school, walking by with her dad! They greet the pair, but some instinct tells them not to invite them to join them, and anyhow, this time is sacred and they like to keep it that way. As they disappear, my friend comments, 'That's nice, they are doing the same thing'. His daughter isn't so sure. She explains, 'Gemma's parents just got divorced. She has to spend weekends with her dad'. Later, when they walk along the street they see the girl and her father sitting in a coffee shop. But they are not talking. He is holding his copy of *The Australian* in front of him like a big wall. His daughter, nursing her coffee mug to her, looks like she would rather be a thousand miles away. It just looks so terribly sad.

A Practice Man

For a girl, Dad is her personal ambassador from the Planet Male. He teaches her what to expect from men. A girl can practise joking, arguing and talking over deep things with Dad, and these skills can carry into her friendships with boys later on. She will be more confident and resistant to manipulation. If her dad treats her with respect, she won't settle for less from the males in her life.

Psychologists have found that mothers and fathers play complementary roles with daughters.[2] Put very simply, mothers make girls SECURE, but dads give them SELF-ESTEEM. Mum supports her daughter like a rock, steady and solid. Dad lifts her up, like a helicopter. If a girl knows that Dad is interested in her, asks her viewpoint about things (and doesn't then argue against them or knock them down) she gets the feeling that she is intelligent, and worthwhile. If he takes her to B&Q on a Saturday to get a glue gun, and stops off for a hot chocolate or ice cream on the way home, she can't avoid the conclusion that she is *interesting for her own sake.* 'He likes my company!' She notices that he is not hurrying, that she is not a task he has to cross off his list. She is the destination.

Actions say it all. Some dads (who might consider themselves good fathers) barely *talk to their daughters,* they merely live in the same house. At least, that's how it feels to the daughter. Other dads have chosen to be a real presence. They check in with her every day, and take time to listen, or even have some regular activity, like walking the dog together, that creates the chance to talk. They enquire about her life. They listen as girls talk about their friends, their projects, what they like and don't like at school. Sometimes there is a kind of ritual: 'What was the worst thing that happened today?', 'What was the best?'

How Not to Fight with Your Teenage Girl

They are smart, they are fast-talking, they are scary, and they live in your house. Teenage girls and dads can fly off the handle with each other – pressing all the wrong buttons – that is, unless dads know about *the inside secrets.*

Here, buried in this book like a special sealed section, is what you need to know.

1. *Your daughter loves you – you've stayed around, been kind and kept her safe and alive for umpteen years. She would be very upset if you were to die, and would miss you forever.*
2. *But all the same, she can find you very irritating. That's because you tend to criticise and find fault, and you do it at the worst times.*

In hundreds of family therapy interviews, trying to find out why a teenage girl is causing trouble, it's come down to this – dads who criticise their daughters, start fights with them and can't accept that they have different points of view. She wants to become her own person, and is acutely sensitive to you trying to control her. So when you lose it, she double loses it, and it all goes haywire. *Daughters have to be treated gently.*

If your daughter wrote you a letter about this, here's what she might say:

Dear Dad

I am a teenager now. It's very hard. My emotions feel like English weather. Life is stressful, what with school and boys and not liking how I look and the mess the world is in and hating my hair.

I need to chill out quite a lot – to watch some TV when I get home from school, and be vague and dreamy and waltz about the house. If you criticise me, it's just kind of the last straw. So I will yell back at you or storm off to my room. But it's not my fault. My prefrontal cortex has melted down for a rebuild and won't be right again until about age 22. So my amygdala has taken over, and all it knows is fight or flight! Scare me and you can choose which one I give you back.

You think because I can out-argue you that I am smart. But I have lost the most important faculty a person can have – I can't see anyone else's point of view. Or at least not easily. It's enough to keep track of my own point of view. In fact I will try on lots of different points of view to find out if one fits. Today I am an emo-punk-Goth-angel and plan to get piercings in my cheeks. Tomorrow I might volunteer as a nurse in Angola.

You worry about boyfriends. You worry about me navigating sex. So do I! We're not on different sides.

You worry that I won't do my schoolwork. Well, how would you feel when they tell you your whole life depends on a couple of days of exams, that it could all be over at 17 if I have a bad night or forget my pen? It's enough to paralyse you with fear.

Please – don't criticise me. I am already criticising myself so much it just might tip me over the edge. And I'd be so upset if I killed you. Talk gently. Ask about my life. Watch the timing, I will sometimes want to talk and sometimes not. When I am, you better have a couple of hours!! Be gentle. Be funny. Be patient. One day I will be over this and we can be the best of friends.

Your (loving) daughter

HEARING HER OUT

In talking with your daughter, allow that sometimes she will be unhappy with you. If you can ask her about what you did wrong, and she tells you, don't try to defend yourself. That's a guy move, and it doesn't work with women or girls. Instead, see if you can figure out the EMOTION she is telling you about. Actually ask her if she is:

sad (you are going away AGAIN),
angry (you didn't keep your word), or
afraid (you drive too fast)

and adjust your actions accordingly. Take a guess and ask her if you have understood her rightly. And then, even though you have been a perfect and impeccably faultless father, try doing something really radical, and admit *you could change a little* to accommodate her. Because (in her view) she has so little power, and you have so much, *if you make changes to your behaviour, or do something that she asks you to do, it makes her feel wonderful that her feelings count.*

More than once in the heat of a painful argument with my daughter during her teens, I would be knocked sideways by the clarity and heartfelt honesty with which she spoke, and how well she was expressing how wrong I was! I'd be caught between wanting to win the argument and being so proud of her, all at the same time.

Speak from the heart and perhaps she will too. The biggest mistake we men make in conflict times is to use 'You … messages'. You are such a slob. You don't help around the house. You are lazy. You are not going out in that dress! But 'I messages' work better. That's because they involve being vulnerable. 'I was scared and worried when you didn't get home at the time you agreed. I need to know I can trust you.' This is not an attack, because it starts with 'I' and not 'You'. It invites her to be caring, not to defend herself. Even 'I am angry because the kitchen was a mess, and I had just tidied it up' is better than 'You messed up the kitchen!'

RESPECT REALLY MATTERS

Sometimes kids learn from TV and the way people talk at school that they can be rude to each other, and you, and that's somehow normal and okay. (In Australia, where I live, a TV sitcom from the UK called *My Family* caused us real astonishment – it seemed to consist of really unpleasant people being horrible to each other. In real life, somebody would commit suicide in a family like that.) Putting people down erodes everyone's happiness and sense of worth. It's perfectly fine to talk it over with the whole family and get an agreement that *nobody talks disrespectfully to anyone else* – parent to child, child to parent, child to child.

It's also important to establish that work has to be shared – cooking, cleaning, laundry, gardening and pets are everyone's responsibility and it's 'fair to share'. Also make sure that your services – driving her to school, helping her in myriad ways – are gladly given but are not to be taken for granted. And they could stop if they are!

Inevitably mistakes will happen, but you will stop and sort it out, say sorry, and gradually make the household a happier place. Rudeness always wounds, and if it becomes normal and accepted, people will be bleeding all the time. Doing your share is a way of saying, love is about what you *do*, not just what you say. She's going to need to know that.

NO MORE PRINCESS

There is a bad mistake that some dads make, especially dads who are money rich but time poor, and that is to treat their daughter like a princess. They buy her expensive gifts and let her have money without earning it. She never has to help around the house, her laundry and meals are all done for her. This leads to an interesting result – a grown-up girl with an emotional age of two. TSO – or terminal self-obsession – is an awful fate for a girl. Tantrums, demands, screeching, breaking things are all evidence that this syndrome has taken hold. The cure is to softly but firmly begin to impose boundaries and also requirements that she pull her weight. Make sure your partner is onside, work out a plan, and get help from a family therapist if you need it to get things on track. This is important, as princesses collide with reality in painful ways if parents don't help them rejoin the human race.

THE MAGIC OF ONE TO ONE

Here is a huge clue to being a dad. While you can have fun with all your children together, *to really be close that time has to be spent one to one*. So sometimes have whole weekends away with just one child. Go somewhere, camp, stay in a cabin, cook, clean, talk, sleep, and you will find you get into a deeper place with each other. Do the same or something different with each child, so they know the joy and memory of having you all to themselves.

BEING CLEARLY NON-SEXUAL

There is a dark side to daughters and dads. A very small number of dads, and stepdads, use their daughters for sexual gratification. This can range from sexual touching through to actual rape.

The problem is not that men can see the attractiveness of their daughter or any girl (but it's wrong to ever act on this, or encourage it in oneself by giving it room in your imagination or nurture it by accessing child porn), the problem is that some men are so psychopathically selfish that they don't draw a line on this. They blur that line or cross it completely. This is always wrong, always harmful and, of course, a crime.

A far wider problem, which probably affects most families, is that by being aware of the problem of sexual abuse, *dads back away from teenage daughters*, not hugging them, not spending time with them, or getting irrationally angry with them for no other reason than that they are starting to look pretty and attractive. Their daughter gets a confusing, hurtful signal that she does not understand: 'he doesn't like me, he doesn't hug me any more, he is weird and uptight around me'. A girl might just feel bad about herself. She might suss out that it's something to do with getting older and more womanly, and try to turn herself back into a little girl again, to be cute and helpless instead of adult and confident in herself.

A dad who is sorted out in his own head about this, who knows how to steer his own attractedness, who is close to his wife and comfortable with his daughter growing up, can affirm her beauty and wit without making her or himself uncomfortable.

Practical Stuff

Start Young

Through her babyhood and toddlerhood, cuddling, swishing her around and playing horsie games on the floor with her helps her to see you as exciting and fun. Be gentle and watch her face to see she is not alarmed.

Gently reading stories or making up stories for her when she is still a toddler, as she is getting ready to fall asleep, gives your wife a spell away from the kids and is a great bonding time.

Being a hands-on dad early makes it so much easier to stay close and develop your relationship as she gets older.

Find Common Interests

Read to her or make up stories when she is small. Find books or characters that you both like. Save her a spot to garden with you. Make things in the shed, go to plays or movies together. Make traditions – 'Me and Dad always do this ...' A common interest like bushwalking or fishing might emerge. Search for the common ground, it will create a lot of good times and great memories.

Listen a Lot

Girls love to talk, so dads need to learn to listen. Enquire about what she is thinking about, dreaming and wishing for in her life. Take her seriously. Ask about what is the best thing that has happened this week. And the worst. When she shares something with you that is private, don't blab it to everyone, apart from possibly her mum. Your daughter needs to know that she can trust you.

Write Notes and Letters

When you are travelling or even just at your workplace, send her notes or an email. Her birthday is a good opportunity to write a card to her letting her know how you feel about her and how proud you are of her. Give lots of examples from the year that has just gone by.

Be a Great Example of Manhood

Be clean, smell good, and dress well around her. Don't swear. Don't tell dirty jokes. Daughters have acute senses, and sensibilities, and even when they are acting rough they don't like it in their father. The way your daughter sees you treat women makes a big difference in how she will see men later in her life. Be on your best behaviour with her, her mother and other female friends and relatives. Simple courtesy and kindness will go a long way in helping her set the bar high for the men in her own life.

IF YOU ARE A SINGLE MUM

It's just possible you are a single mum reading this. You could be feeling bad that your daughter doesn't have a dad she knows, or who is around very much in her life. I've talked to hundreds of single mums and daughters of single mums, and here is what they have told me helps with this problem:

1. Recruit men you can really trust to be interested in her, teach her, and spend time with her. Grandfathers and uncles will be cautious about showing an interest, especially when she is in her teens, but if you ask them, she will benefit from their teaching her to do things, talking and laughing with her, being involved in her life. *(Don't leave her with grown-up men on her own, but stay nearby, and both will feel safer and more at ease.)* Men often need to be asked, it engages their 'practical help' gene and they do a great job.
2. You yourself are a big role model. If you are angry and disappointed with men, she may be ambivalent, either feeling the same, or flipping to the other extreme and being man crazy. It's important that you get help for any issues about being hurt by men, and that you relate to men with strength and dignity, but warmth too, so that she sees you can get along with men. If you re-partner, do it slowly and cautiously, with a lot of care. But don't do it unless you yourself feel really ready. Being strongly and happily single is also a good example for her in emotional independence.

What Happened to Kaycee?

Remember Kaycee? I promised to let you know how things worked out for her, so here goes. When Kaycee's parents heard her story, right there in the counsellor's room, they both were in tears. It was suddenly and painfully clear that they had really not been as close to their daughter, or known her inner world, anywhere near as much as she had needed. Both mother and father began, in the weeks that followed, and with the counsellor's help, to work out how to set this right. It had taken years for the problem to develop, and it would be best to go carefully and with determination to make it right.

Kaycee's mum had a small business, a group of fashion shops, which absorbed much of her time and energy and had done so since her children were small. She resolved that this had taken up too much of her time – she had two younger children as well as Kaycee and was also concerned for them. She rearranged her life, with one clear goal: that she would be home when the kids came home from school. From that basis, she would begin to build a stronger connection with them. She made no promises or fanfare about this, it just simply began to happen, but it was close to 100 per cent. It changed the entire feeling of their family life.

(In telling you this story, I am aware that you might well ask, why was it the mother who had to curtail her career? All I can say is this is what this mother decided. Life isn't always ideologically right.)

Kaycee's father was, if anything, more distraught. He wanted to break heads, phone lawyers. But he was led to understand that this was in a way the easy route – throw some power around. What was needed was harder than that. He acknowledged, painfully and slowly, that he had been a woeful father, at least on a personal level. He too began to work out ways in which he could listen, attend and show up more in his children's lives.

This dad travelled a lot with work, and it occurred to him that an upcoming job in Cairns, in tropical north Queensland, would occur during Kaycee's mid-year break and that potentially she could come with him, and perhaps go snorkelling for a few days on the reef afterwards. He put this idea to Kaycee, fully expecting she would snub the idea, that the last thing she'd want to do would be hang out with an old guy like him.

So he was surprised when she said 'yes', and looked and sounded genuinely keen. In fact, she looked vulnerable, as if thinking, 'Will it really happen? Will he cancel at the last minute?' Kaycee was taking a risk, they both were vulnerable to it being a failure and they might not get along. That's how it is with real relationships, your heart is on the line.

The trip went well. The business part took three days so Kaycee was blissed out to lie by the pool, wander around the promenade and shops, and read books. She also had the chance to observe her father in a work setting. She saw that it was not all smooth sailing, that he was under pressure, dealing with a lot, rallying a lot of energy. She realised that this was something he did every day, so as to provide for his family. But at the same time she saw that he had talents and skills and was using them for a good end. It was a side of him she hadn't seen.

Then they travelled up to Port Douglas, the Barrier Reef, and the fun part. At least that was the plan. On the first night, something small happened, a little flare up over tidying up, Kaycee can't really remember what it was, but suddenly they were fighting and out it all came. (Perhaps you've experienced this, a small issue suddenly provides the detonator for the main explosion – all the hurts and resentments built up over months or years come bursting out.)

Kaycee really let fly. It was very specific – the time in Grade 4 when she had been the solo singer in the concert. He had promised to come, and not shown up. A time he had yelled at her mother, frightening them all. But mostly his absence, his distractedness around the house, his preference for the shelter of his newspaper than the games and interests of his children.

Dave, the father, fought a huge urge to defend himself, to give reasons, to counterattack with examples of her selfishness, her deficiencies as a daughter. He kept a tight rein on this, breathed deeply and kept listening. In fact, he asked for more information, more details. And Kaycee kept it coming!

As she wound down, she was aware of his face, and a look of remorse mixed with a kind of pride almost in her gutsiness. This wasn't a tantrum, there was real hurt and vulnerability in what she was saying. He was genuinely ashamed of causing her so much pain. That look spoke to her more than words, and the feeling between them softened.

The next day, swimming among the turtles and multi-hued corals, was beautiful. They chatted to other tourists. The days flew past. Father and daughter, still tentative and careful, found themselves laughing or just spending sweet quiet time, wordlessly happy to just be.

When they got home Kaycee's mum couldn't wait to ask her how it had been. She waited until there was a good time, peaceful and private. Later that night, she spoke to Dave about it as they lay in bed. 'You know, Dave, there's something I want you to hear. I don't think Kaycee would mind. I asked Kaycee how the trip had gone. She told me, *those were the best six days of her life*.'

Special Bonus Section: Where Do I Go from Here?

I really hope that this book has addressed every question and filled every need you have as a mum, dad or carer raising a girl. That it stays on your bedside table as a friendly resource and helps you often in the years to come.

Some readers though, may have a feeling of needing more. The next step, when a book doesn't help, is to get individual help, counselling or therapy, but that's not always easy. So once this book was written, I set to work with a team of people, including some of the best educators and girl experts around the world, to create some 'stronger medicine' – a follow-up book which would be like intensive therapy or a small group workshop. This book is called *10 Things Girls Need Most*.

10 Things Girls Need Most is a diagnostic book that helps you look at your unique girl, in close-up detail, whatever her age, and analyse what she needs, what strengths she has, where she might be in danger and what is missing from her life that you can begin to augment. It is partly a workbook – you complete questionnaires and make new insights and connections, just as happens in therapy. Bring your own tissues! And it's also full of actions you can bring into your home and your family.

10 Things Girls Need Most also does what a therapist does – it looks at your girlhood if you are a mum, or your boyhood if you are a dad, to see where you might have been damaged, and then looks at the family dynamic you have created – if you are too busy, too stressed, or need more boundaries, if you need to be happier and more playful – so that your daughter can have a better childhood than you did.

Do have a look at *10 Things Girls Need Most* in a library or bookstore and see if it might help you even more. It's also a great resource for discussion with friends or, if you work with parents, for setting up a course or programme.

To give you one last gift from the pages of this book, I've condensed the basic idea into a bonus section right here.

What Are the Ten Things Girls Need Most?

You might ask – who says there are only ten? Or which ten? I agree, but it's a helpful way to sort out the terrible blur of confusion we find often ourselves in with parenthood. Decades of mental health research has shown there are some definitive pillars of mental health for young people (many of these apply to boys too).

Thinking about your daughter or daughters, consider which of these you think they have in their life, which ones are a 'maybe' and which are really not happening. And perhaps some of them can be revved up, once you know how much they matter.

IMPORTANT NOTE: very few girls would ever achieve or receive all ten. Don't use this list as a reason to feel bad. (For example, a third of all girls don't have a dad active or engaged in their lives at some time. That just means that at some stage it will help to find safe, respectful men – granddads, uncles, school teachers, the gay man next door – who care about them as an individual). Perfection is impossible, and you wouldn't like it anyway. Do your best.

For each of the following, tick the answer that comes closest.

1. A secure and loving start

In the early years kids learn to trust the world and feel secure in it. There are parts of their brain that grow best when we are loving, take things at a gentle pace and delight in their company. So we need to slow down, do less, and be peaceful around babies and toddlers. Yet often this is the most stressed time of our lives! Caring for young parents is something our society, our economy and our politicians seem to do less and less well. But luckily, if you had a stressful time in your daughter's early years, it's not too late now to rebuild calming and nurturing into your family life. It starts with an honest appraisal:

How stressed were her first two years?
- VERY
- SOMETIMES
- NOT AT ALL – THEY WERE PRETTY GOOD!

2. The chance to be wild, and time to be a child

This means spending time in nature, even if it's just a backyard with a few trees to climb, pets, going for walks, making a mess with mud and leaves, spending loads of free time without screens or devices, organised activities or pressures. Being noisy and free. Not having to grow up too soon, be sexy or worry about looks or be caught up with social media. Well into her teens, being free to be herself and not conform or fit in with narrow ideas of what a girl should be or do.

How free and natural and happy is your daughter's girlhood?
- NOT VERY
- A BIT
- VERY

3. Friendship skills

Getting along with others is hard. It has to be learned, mostly in the primary school years, by lots of discussion with mum or dad or other trusted adults, while being in the fray with her peer group every day at school. (There are seven friendship skills explored in the new book. My favourite two are: 'you can be friends with someone and not always agree – or always want to do what they do', and 'some people haven't learned to be trustworthy yet – so don't trust them with what is precious to you'. (Wouldn't it have been great to have known those two when you were a kid?)

Has your daughter been able to learn how to get along with friends and people in general?
- NOT VERY WELL
- A BIT
- YES, SHE IS GOOD AT THIS FOR HER AGE

4. Backbone and strength

When we take a firm line with our daughters and encourage them to do hard things that require persistence, care for others and not always take the easy route, they grow a backbone. They learn to handle hardship, delay rewards and do the hard but right thing. They develop a clear idea of right and wrong and a sense of justice, and become brave in standing up for others.

Does your daughter have backbone?
- NO, SHE IS EASILY SWAYED AND NOT VERY STRONG
- A BIT
- YES, SHE DOES

5. Spark, and a reason to be alive

Spark is another word for an interest or passion that is consuming and life-enhancing – something that draws out your daughter's enthusiasm and creativity. It can be anything from music to animals, karate to crochet. Sadly, many kids lose their spark, or never even discover it, and it's our job to help find and support it. When your daughter has a spark in her life this is a major mental health pillar because it gives her a reason to be alive beyond mere fitting in. And it engages her with older people and often sets her direction in life.

Does your daughter have an interest – something that she loves to do, and which brings out the best in her?
- NO
- A BIT
- DEFINITELY

6. The love and respect of a dad

Dads are the opposite sex, and for most girls that's the gender they will be interested in partnering with and will interact with for better or worse, all their life. So the interest and love of a father (or someone else in their stead) is very important, if not crucial, to their self-esteem. A girl should feel that she is special and irreplaceably important to her dad. Very few women who grew up in the twentieth century were sure of that in their own growing up, and we are still healing those wounds today.

Does your daughter have a caring, involved father who spends lots of time with her, and doesn't give up even if he gets it wrong sometimes?
- NO
- SOMEWHAT
- DEFINITELY

7. Aunties, and a rite of passage

Around the age of 12, a girl often decides 'I don't want to turn into my mum!' Which is sad for us, but an important part of her becoming strong and free. But she needs adults just as much, and this is where aunties or auntie-surrogates come in. Aunties talk straight – they are more cool than mum, or at least, different, and they make her feel secure in a different way. A favourite auntie will have her over to stay sometimes, have a regular lunch date with her in her teens, ask her views, challenge her thinking and set her straight about boys and men!

Does your daughter have another woman than you in her life? Someone she can confide in, and be challenged by, as she grows up?
- NO
- SOMEWHAT
- DEFINITELY

8. A happy sexuality

We've had a sexual revolution, and now girls are allowed to know about sex, enjoy it, and be in charge of when and with who it happens. So why is it becoming such a disaster area? Pornography is miseducating boys, who have become rushed, terrible lovers who forget that girls are human beings too. And pop culture teaches girls they are a decoration, there to please boys, and sex is another performance you have to be amazing at. So we're going backwards. But some girls are great, they are in charge, they know it's fine to enjoy the stage they are at – and are happy and alive in their bodies. A happy sexuality is one where you go at your own pace, for your own age, and you call the shots.

Is your daughter – for her age
- INSECURE AND MISUSED?
- PRETTY GOOD?
- STRONG AND HAPPY IN HER BODY?

9. Feminism
Women used to think there was something wrong with them if they didn't like cooking scones and cleaning house. Or being bored in bed. Or being put down or hit. Or being unsafe in the streets. Our daughters need to know about this – that it's better to be angry than afraid, and it's together that we are strong. They need to know they are in a war and it's not over yet.

Does your daughter:
- SEE ALL HER PROBLEMS AS INDIVIDUAL ONES?
- SUSPECT THIS HAPPENS TO OTHERS TOO?
- REALISE THAT EVERYWHERE IN THE WORLD GIRLS AND WOMEN STILL HAVE TERRIBLE LIVES, AND HER PROBLEMS ARE A PART OF A LARGER FIGHT?

10. Spirit
Do you know what the world today teaches our kids? 'You are on your own, happiness is something you buy, life is a contest and the winner takes all.' All of which are life-destroying lies. Suicide is the ultimate end point of this kind of aloneness, but there's lots of misery along the way.

Little children and wise adults know that they are part of nature, connected to everything that lives and breathes, and that love runs through life like a hidden river keeping us sustained and sustaining. However you understand spirituality, it's the key to life itself.

Does your daughter
- FEEL VERY ALONE IN THE WORLD?
- FEEL THAT PERHAPS THERE IS CONNECTION?
- KNOW THAT SHE IS PART OF CREATION AND LOVE WILL ALWAYS BE THERE?

These have been deeply inadequate explanations of profound things, but hopefully they have started you thinking. Deep down, you have known these things, but now they are at your fingertips, in clear sight.

Look back at your answers. How many times did you tick the first option? Could you choose one of those and do something about it? Would that be a key to your daughter's life turning around? If you want to explore more, *10 Things Girls Need Most* is our very best effort to put this in a helpful, beautiful way, worthy of the girl you love.

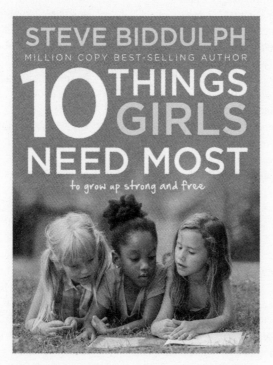

Notes

Dear Reader

Most people don't read this part of the book. However, I have tried to tell the story of why these sources are included, and a bit more background, so you might find it worth a skim.

A Flight Manual for Your Girl

1. Gunnell, D., Kidger, J. and Elvidge, H. (2018), 'Adolescent mental health in crisis', *British Medical Journal*, available at https://www.bmj.com/content/361/bmj.k2608.full; Robinson, E., Power, L. and Allan, D., 'What works with adolescents? Family connections and involvement in interventions for adolescent problem behaviours', AFRC Briefing 16 March 2010, Australian Institute of Family Studies, available at https://aifs.gov.au/cfca/publications. Here is a key quote:

   'Close relationships with parents can be a protective factor against poor outcomes. Part of this protective relationship is the "secure base" function that parents continue to play in the adolescent years

(Daniel et al., 1999; particularly mothers – see Markiewicz et al., 2006). Five elements of a secure parent- or caregiver-adolescent attachment have been described in the literature (Schofield & Beek, 2009):

- availability – helping young people to trust;
- sensitivity – helping young people to manage feelings and behaviours;
- acceptance – building the self-esteem of the young person;
- co-operation – helping young people to feel effective; and
- family membership – helping young people belong.'

Meet Kaycee and Genevieve

1. A good overview of the mental health crisis affecting young people is Eckersley, R. (2011), 'Troubled Youth: An Island of Misery in a Sea of Happiness, or the Tip of an Iceberg of Suffering?', *Intervention in Psychiatry*, 5 (Suppl. 1): 6–11. Also Henshaw, S., *The Triple Bind: Saving our Teenage Girls from Today's Pressures*, Ballantine, 2009, gives stunning

incidence figures for rising suicide, violence, mental health admissions, self-harm, alcohol and eating disorder problems for girls worldwide. Henshaw is Professor of Psychology at UC Berkeley.

1: Creating a Total Girl

1. The research on gender differences is vast, and they have been both understated and overstated at different times. A good introduction for parents to brain differences in girls is Nagel, M., *It's a Girl Thing*, Hawker Brownlow, 2008. A timely warning on not overstating gender differences is Fine, C., *Delusions of Gender*, Icon, 2010. This book reminds us that while there are gender differences in predisposition, these are 'soft-wired' and we can greatly influence them to ensure no disadvantage or limitations are put on either gender.

2: Right from the Start

1. The importance of mother–child attunement is discussed with great clarity in Manne, A., *Motherhood: How Should We Care for Our Children?*, Allen & Unwin, 2005. An encouraging and affecting read for anyone who wants to think more deeply about being a parent in a society that doesn't make that easy. For more of the science on joint attention sequences see Carpenter, M., Nagell, K. *et al.*

(1998), 'Social Cognition, Joint Attention, and Communicative Competence from 9 to 15 Months of Age', *Monographs of the Society for Research in Child Development*, 63(4), i+iii+v–vi+1–174.

2. Seligman, M., *Helplessness: On Depression, Development and Death*, 1975. Seligman went on to found the field of Positive Psychology. Leaving babies to cry themselves out is a concern to many in the infant attachment field, because it endangers the sense of trust between parent and child. There are some great books on gentler ways to help children sleep, such as Sears, W., and Sears, M., *The Baby Sleep Book*, Little Brown, 2005. And the excellent Australian book Gethin, A., and Macgregor, B., *Helping Your Baby to Sleep*, Finch, 2012.

3. A great summary of father–child interaction studies is in Fletcher, R., *The Dad Factor*, Finch, 2011. Richard heads the Family Action Centre at the University of Newcastle – google him there for research articles. He has done pioneering work with indigenous dads, dads in prison, and dads with postnatal depression.

4. Paley, Vivian Gussin, *A Child's World: The Importance of Fantasy Play*, University of Chicago Press, 2005. This acclaimed book explains how important, rich, and healing children's make-believe play really is, and how to encourage it. A textbook in many

courses, you can often get it cheaply second-hand.

3: Learning to Explore

1. Degotardi, S. (ed.), *ECH13 Play and Inquiry in Early Childhood*, Macquarie University/Pearson, 2011. Good overview of the play research field. Fivush, R., Brotman, M. A., Buckner, J. P. and Goodman, S. H. (2000), 'Gender Differences in Parent–Child Emotion Narratives', *Sex Roles* 42(3–4): 233–253. doi: 10.1023/a:10007091207068.

2. Mary Ainsworth's work in Uganda in the 1950s established for the first time that patterns between mother and baby are universal across all cultures. With John Bowlby she founded attachment theory, the basis of our whole understanding of how children thrive. (Of course, indigenous people had known this for 300,000 years.) This article is just one of hundreds she wrote. Ainsworth, M. (1989), 'Attachments Beyond Infancy', *American Psychologist*, 44(4) April: 709–716.

3. Kim Payne's message about simplifying life for children and restoring their rhythms of activity and rest is something the world urgently needs to hear. Payne, K. J., and Ross, L. M., *Simplicity Parenting*, Ballantine 2010. Also a good website with many resources: www.simplicityparenting.com. The wider movement to protect, slow down, and deepen the experience of childhood is authoritatively explored by many leading voices in House, R., (ed.), *Too Much Too Soon*, Hawthorn Press, 2011.

4. A fuller description of how to use 'stand and think' safely and kindly with children is in Biddulph, S. and S., *The Complete Secret of Happy Children*, and also in *More Secrets of Happy Children*, HarperCollins Australia/Thorsons UK, 2006.

4: Getting Along with Others

1. Here's a nice change – a wonderful DVD from New Zealand called *Untouchable Girls: Topp Twins the Movie*. A moving story with many performances, both comedic and musical. Available at www.topptwins.com.

2. Gurian, M., *The Wonder of Girls*, Atria, 2002. This book divides people greatly. It's thoughtful, and deep, and the Gurians are engaged parents and give detailed help on many aspects of girlhood. But it occasionally wanders wildly into what many read as biological determinism. If you are the kind of person who has friends they love but sometimes disagree with, you will be able to take the good and leave what you don't like.

3. Thompson, M., and Grace, C., *Best Friends, Worst Enemies: Understanding the Social Lives of Children*, Ballantine, 2001. This

book is almost up there with Penelope Leach in its close-up knowledge of the world of children. One big benefit of the book can be summed up in this quote: 'In my experience what interferes most strongly with a parent's wisdom in this area are the painful memories from his or her own childhood.' Very helpful in *not overreacting*.

4. David, D. and Lyons, R. K. (2005), 'Differential Attachment Responses of Male and Female Infants to Frightening Maternal Behaviour: Tend and Befriend vs. Fight or Flight?', *Infant Mental Health Journal*, 21(1): 1–18. If you are really into this stuff, www. parentingscience.com/strange-situation.html as well as the whole website, is a treasure trove of good science applied to parenthood.

5: Finding Her Soul

1. To hear Peter Benson's inspiring and moving talk on spark, go to Youtube and search under Benson and spark. It's actually a TED talk. Peter's book, Benson, P., *Sparks: How Parents Can Ignite the Hidden Strengths of teenagers*, Jossey-Bass, 2008, includes quizzes, questionnaires and other research based materials to help you and your child find their spark and follow it through. http://www.search-institute.org/sparks

2. Okay, fasten your seatbelt. The concerns about hormone disruptors in everyday items like plastics, air fresheners and supermarket dockets are so great, I have included far more documentation.

First – that it's happening ... Euling, S., *et al.* (1 February 2008), 'Examination of US Puberty-Timing Data from 1940 to 1994 for Secular Trends: Panel Findings', *Pediatrics*, 121, Supplement 3: pp. S172–S191 and also Golub, M. S., Collman, G. W., Foster, P. *et al.* (1 February 2008), 'Public Health Implications of Altered Puberty Timing', *Pediatrics*, 121, Supplement 3: pp. S218–S230.

Second – that it's a problem ... Children with early puberty are at a risk for accelerated skeletal maturation and short adult height, early sexual debut, potential sexual abuse, and psychosocial difficulties. Altered puberty timing is also of concern for the development of reproductive tract cancers later in life. For example, an early age of menarche is a risk factor for breast cancer. Altered timing of puberty also has implications for behavioural disorders. For example, an early maturation is associated with a greater incidence of conduct and behaviour disorders during adolescence. Finally, altered puberty timing is considered an adverse effect in reproductive toxicity risk assessment for chemicals. Recent US legislation has mandated improved chemical testing approaches for protecting children's health and screening for endocrine-disrupting agents (ibid.).

Thirdly, that BPA and Pthalates have a powerful effect on babies and children, especially when exposure happens in pregnancy.

3. 'Impact of Early Life Bisphenol A Exposure on Behaviour and Executive Function in Children', Braun, J. M. *et al.*, *Paediatrics Online*, 24 October 2011. *In utero* exposure to the organic compound bisphenol A (BPA), widely used in the manufacture of plastics, including cups and food containers, was associated with *behaviour disruptions at age 3*, particulary among girls. Increased gestational exposure to BPA also was associated with *higher depression* scores in girls. For each tenfold increase in gestational urinary BPA concentration, there was an adjusted increase in *anxiety scores* according to Joe M. Braun, PhD, of the Harvard School of Public Health in Boston, and colleagues. The increase was pronounced among girls but minimal among boys, the researchers reported online in *Pediatrics*. Braun and colleagues had previously found that gestational exposure was associated with *hyperactivity and aggressive behaviour* in girls aged 2.

4. 'A 2008 study published in the *Journal of American Medicine* looked at urinary BPA levels in 1,455 US adults. The result: The higher the BPA concentration in people's urine, the higher their incidence of *cardiovascular trouble and diabetes*': Lang, I. A., Galloway, T.S. *et al.* (17 September 2008), 'Association of Urinary Bisphenol A Concentration with Medical Disorders and Laboratory Abnormalities in Adults', *JAMA*, 300(11): 1303–10. Epub 2008 16 September 2008.

And what to do … Previous research has suggested that avoiding food packaged in plastic may lessen the impact, advice that was echoed by Braun and colleagues. Canned soup was identified as a particular concern. 'The FDA's own research shows that BPA leaches from can linings into food, and a 2011 Harvard study found BPA at heightened levels in people who regularly consume canned soup'. And it doesn't take much …

5. Carwile, J, Luu, H, *et al.*, 'Use of Polycarbonate Bottles and Urinary Bisphenol A Concentrations', *Environmental Health Perspectives*, online 12 May 2009. A Harvard study supports what many public health specialists have long assumed: Hard plastic drinking bottles containing Bisphenol A are leaching notable amounts of the controversial chemical into

people's bodies. And here's some more just in case you're in any doubt: Caserta, D., Maranghi. L., and Mantovani, A. (2008), 'Impact of Endocrine Disruptor Chemicals in Gynaecology', *Human Reproduction Update*, 14(1):59–72; Sathyanarayana, S. (February 2008), 'Phthalates and Children's Health: Current Problems', *Pediatric and Adolescent Health Care*, 38: 34–49; Vandenberg, L. N., Hauser, R., Marcus, M. *et al.* (2007), 'Human Exposure to Bisphenol A (BPA), *Reproductive Toxicology*, 24: 139–177; Austen, Ian (19 April 2008), 'Canada Takes Steps to Ban Most Plastic Baby Bottles', *New York Times*; Colon, I., Caro, D., Bourdony, C.J., Rosario, O. (2000), 'Identification of Phthalate Esters in the Serum of Young Puerto Rican Girls with Premature Breast Development', *Environ Health Perspect* 108: 895–900; Reddy, B. S., Rozati, R., Reddy, B. V., Raman, N. V. (May 2006), 'Association of Phthalate Esters with Endometriosis in Indian Women', *BJOG*, 113(5): 515–20.

6. The poem appears in Pallotta-Chiarolli, M., *When Our Children Come Out*, Finch, 2005. More of Pamela's poems are at www. angelfire.com/pq/pam/poems. html

7. Wolfson, Amy R., and Carskadon, Mary A. (2003), 'Understanding Adolescents' Sleep Patterns and School Performance: A Critical Appraisal', *Sleep Medicine Review*, 7(6): 491–506.; Carskadon, M.A. (ed.). *Adolescent Sleep Patterns: Biological, Social, and Psychological Influences*, Cambridge University Press, Cambridge, 2002; Wolfson, Amy R., and Carskadon, Mary A. (1998), 'Sleep Schedules and Daytime Functioning in Adolescents', *Child Development*, 69: 875–887; *JSTOR*, 19 October 2005; Owens, J., Belon, K. and Moss, P. (2010), 'Impact of Delaying School Start Time on Adolescent Sleep, Mood, and Behavior', *Archives of Pediatrics and Adolescent Medicine* 164(7): 608–614.

6: Preparing for Adulthood

1. An excellent resource website for girls entering and moving through puberty is www. ritesforgirls.com. The founder, Kim McCabe, is a youth worker and mother who has thought deeply about these questions and developed a special puberty group approach, and helps others start similar groups.

2. This segment draws from a feature article entitled 'Out of the Dark' by journalist Chris Johnston. It appeared in *Good Weekend* magazine, 19 May 2012. A similar article with additional information appeared in the *Sunday Tasmanian*. Also Adams, C., 'Missy Higgins' Secret Musical Crisis', *Herald Sun*, 4 April 2012.

7: The Rush We're All in

1. McCabe, K., *From Daughter to Woman*, Robinson, 2018.
2. Lam, T., Lenton, S., et al. (2016) 'Most recent risky drinking session with Australian teenagers' *Australian and New Zealand Journal of Public Health*, https://doi.org/10.1111/1753-6405.12598
3. Skinner, S. R., Robinson, M., Smith, M. A. *et al.* (2015), 'Childhood Behavior Problems and Age at First Sexual Intercourse: A Prospective Birth Cohort Study', *Pediatrics* 135/2. Ten per cent of girls have had sex before age 15, and 25 per cent before age 16. This goes against the wider trend, worldwide, of teenagers having less early sex, and lower rates of pregnancy. The article suggests that there are unique risk factors that are creating this counter-trend subgroup.

8: Too Sexy Too Soon

1. Crawford, S., 'Boys Accused of Raping Girl Too Young to Understand It Was Wrong', *The Daily Telegraph*, Sydney, 21 September 2017.
2. Jeffreys, B., 'Mothers Want Action Over Sexual Assaults at School', *BBC News Online*, 13 September 2018; official report of the Women and Equalities Select Committee into sexual harassment and sexual violence in schools, 2015: https://publications.parliament.uk/pa/cm201617/cmselect/cmwomeq/91/9105.htm#_idTextAnchor010
3. Yeo, H. M. and Yeo W. W. (1993), 'Repeat Deliberate Self-harm: a Link with Childhood Sexual Abuse?' *Archives of Emergency Medicine*, 10(3): 161–166.
4. Bates, L., 'Are We Ignoring an Epidemic of Sexual Violence in Schools?', *Guardian*, 12 December 2017.
5. Agius, P. A., Pitts, M. K., *et al.* (2010), Australian Research Centre in Sex, Health and Society, 'Sexual Behavior and Related Knowledge Among a Representative Sample of Secondary School Students Between 1997 and 2008', *Australian and New Zealand Journal of Public Health*, 34(5): 476–481. The marked increase in students, particularly those in Year 12, having sexual intercourse with multiple partners is also significant. Factors such as early age of sexual debut and relationship formation, and increased alcohol consumption have been associated with increases in the number of sexual partnerships of adolescents ... and these may also *be symptomatic of a more broader cultural change in adolescent sexuality and identity. In Australia, rates of alcohol consumption among secondary students have increased markedly, as has the proportion of young people engaging in sex while*

under the influence of alcohol or drugs ...

6. The best and most moving descriptions of how community and adult connectedness has disappeared for our girls come from the books of Mary Pipher. Highly recommended: Pipher, M., *Reviving Ophelia: Saving the Selves of Adolescent Girls*, Ballantine, 2002; Pipher, M., *The Shelter of Each Other*, Riverhead, 2008.

7. Large, M., *Set Free Childhood*, Hawthorn Press, 2003. Excellent summary of the research into children and media. Deals especially well with the brain and developmental harms of too many screens and too passive use of playing time. Its a popular book aimed at parents.

8. 'Media Guidelines for Parents' (n.d.), American Academy of Pediatrics. Retrieved 24 August 2006, from: http://www.aap.org/pubed/ZZZGVL4PQ7C.htm?,"_cat=17. The American Academy of Pediatrics recommends no more than one to two hours of quality TV and videos a day for older children and no screen time for children under the age of 2. They also specify that parents should: 'Keep TV sets, VCRs, video games and computers out of children's bedrooms.'

9. Tolman, D., *Dilemmas of Desire: Teenage Girls Talk About Sexuality*, Harvard University Press, 2005. This is an excellent book for parents wanting to be life-affirming rather than negative in their approach to their daughter's sexuality.

9: Mean Girls

1. Australia's National Centre Against Bullying is a superb resource for schools, parents and children. www.ncab.org.au. Some statistics:

   • One student in every four in Australian schools is affected by bullying.

   • Kids who are bullied are three times more likely to show depressive symptoms, says the Centre for Adolescent Health.

   • Children who were bullied were up to nine times more likely to have suicidal thoughts, say some studies.

   • Girls who were victims of bullying in their early primary school years were more likely to remain victims as they got older, according to British research.

   • Children who were frequently bullied by their peers were more likely to develop psychotic symptoms in their early adolescence, says more UK research.

   • Girls were much more likely than boys to be victims of both cyber and traditional bullying, says a recent Murdoch Children's Research Institute study.

   • Children as young as three can become victims of

bullying, says Canadian research.

- Young people who bully have a one in four chance of having a criminal record by the age of 30.
- Bullying is the fourth most common reason young people seek help from children's help services.

2. See above.
3. And a good guide to changing the culture and climate in schools to reduce bullying: Cross, D., Thompson, S., Waters, S., Pearce, N., Thomas, L. (2012), *Friendly Schools Plus Evidence for Practice*, STEPS Professional Development, ISBN 978 1 021321.
4. Wiseman, R., *Queen Bees and Wannabes: Helping Your Daughter Survive Cliques, Gossip, Boyfriends and the New Realities of Girl World*, Three Rivers Press, 2009. Rosalind also has an excellent website with a great deal of video content: www.rosalindwiseman.com.
5. Long, J., Long, N. and Whitson, S., *The Angry Smile: The New Psychological Study of Passive Aggressive Behavior at Home, at School, in Marriages and Close Relationships, in the Workplace and Online*, Pro Ed, 2017.
6. This idea came from Maggie's talk, 'What's happening to our girls?' Maggie's book is Hamilton, M., *What's Happening to Our Girls?* Viking Penguin, 2009. Also a wonderful book for girls, a practical, networking and ideas

book about being creative, with beautiful inspiring ideas for making and doing, interspersed with wise help, is Hamilton, M., *Secret Girls' Business*, Penguin, 2012.
7. Brady, N., 'Empathy Tactic Fails on Worst Bullies', *The Age*, 19 August 2012. Reports on research to be released by Kate Hadwen's team in late 2012.

10: Bodies, Weight and Food

1. The National Eating Disorders Collaboration website: http://www.nedc.com.au/eating-disorders-explained
2. See above.
3. Bacon, Linda, *Health At Every Size: The Surprising Truth About Your Weight*. BenBella Books, San Francisco, 2010.
4. Bacon, L. and Aphramor, L. (2011), 'Weight Science: Evaluating the Evidence for a Paradigm Shift', *Nutrition Journal Online*, 10: 69. doi:10.1186/1475–2891–10–9.
5. Priya, S., Prendergast, L., Delbridge, E., Purcell, K., Shulkes, A., Kriketos, A., Proietto, J. (2011), 'Long-term Persistence of Hormonal Adaptations to Weight Loss', *New England Journal of Medicine*, 365: 1597–1604.
6. Neumark-Sztainer, D., Wall, M., Guo, J., Story, M., Haines, J., Eisenberg, M. (2006), 'Obesity, Disordered Eating, and Eating Disorders in a Longitudinal Study of Adolescents: How Do Dieters

Fare 5 Years Later?' *J Am Diet Assoc.*, 106: 559–568.

7. Field, A., Austin, S., Taylor, C., Malspeis, S., Rosner, B., Rockett, H., Colditz, G. A., (2003) 'Relation Between Dieting and Weight Change among Preadolescents and Adolescents', *Paediatrics*, 112(4): 900–6.

8. National Eating Disorders Collaboration (2011). Retrieved 2 August 2012 from http://www.beactive.wa.gov.au/assets/files/Guidelines/Evaluating%20the%20Risk%20of%20Harm180311%20FINAL.pdf.

9. Lumeng, J., Forrest, P., Appugliese, D., Kaciroti, N., Corwyn, R., Bradley, R. (2010), 'Weight Status as a Predictor of Being Bullied in Third through Sixth Grades', *Paediatrics*, 125(6), 1301–7.

10. O'Dea, J. (2005), 'Prevention of child obesity: "First, do no harm"', *Health Education Research*, 20(2): 259–265.

11. Turner, Lydia, (9 July 2010), 'Look Good by Doing Very Little', Australian Broadcasting Corporation, *The Drum*. Retrieved from http://www.abc.net.au/unleashed/36460.html.

12. Treasure, J., Tchanturia, K., Schmidt, U. (2005), 'Developing a Model of the Treatment for Eating Disorders: Using Neuroscience Research to Examine the How Rather than the What of Change', *Counselling and Psychotherapy Research*, 5(3): 1–12.

13. Ibid.

14. Bacon, Linda, *Health At Every Size: The Surprising Truth About Your Weight*, BenBella Books, 2010.

15. Ibid.

16. National Eating Disorders Association, 'The Impact of Media Images on Body Image and Behaviours: A Summary of the Scientific Evidence' (press release), retrieved 2 August 2012 from www.nationaleatingdisorders.org/uploads

17. Grabe, S., Ward, M., Hyde, J. (2008), 'The Role of the Media in Body Image Concerns Among Women: a Meta-analysis of Experimental and Correlational Studies', *Psychological Bulletin*, 134(3): 460–476.

11: Alcohol and Other Drugs

1. I'm grateful to Paul Dillon for his help in writing this chapter and providing the statistics and examples. Paul's website is www.darta.net.au.

2. Dillon, P., *Teenagers, Alcohol and Drugs*, Allen & Unwin, 2009. Excellent and eye-opening book about what are the real concerns, and what are not. Positive, easy to read and with many stories. We need to know about what our kids encounter if we are to help them.

3. Alcohol manufacturers, retailers, and shareholders profit from causing untold harm to our young, according to researchers

and public health campaigners. This article sums up the advertising impacts on teen drinking. The marketing of alcohol to the young should be made illegal. www. generationnext.com. au/2012/08/ how-alcohol-ads-target-kids/14 August 2012.

Parents might do their best to shield their kids from advertising related to alcohol, but alcohol marketers are doing their best to reach them anyway. That's the finding of new research that discovered that the content of alcohol ads placed in magazines is more likely to violate industry guidelines if the ad appears in a magazine with sizable youth readership.

The research, which was done by the Center on Alcohol Marketing and Youth (CAMY) at the Johns Hopkins Bloomberg School of Public Health, found that ads in magazines with a substantial youth readership (15 per cent or more) frequently showed alcohol being consumed in an irresponsible manner. Examples include showing alcohol consumption near or on bodies of water, encouraging overconsumption, and providing messages supportive of alcohol addiction. In addition, nearly one in five ad occurrences contained sexual connotations or sexual objectification.

As at least 14 studies have found that the more young people are exposed to alcohol advertising and marketing, the more likely they are to drink, or if already drinking, to drink more, this report should serve as a wake-up call to parents and everyone else concerned about the health of young people.

The researchers examined 1,261 ads for alcopops, beer, spirits or wine that appeared more than 2,500 times in 11 different magazines that have or are likely to have disproportionately youthful readerships. Ads were analysed for different risk codes: injury content, overconsumption content, addiction content, sex-related content and violation of industry guidelines. This latter category refers to the voluntary codes of good marketing practice administered by alcohol industry trade associations.

According to CAMY, alcohol is responsible for 4,700 deaths per year among young people under the age of 21, and is associated with the three leading causes of death among youth: motor vehicle crashes, homicide and suicide.

12: Mirror, Mirror on the Screen

1. Mineo, L., 'Good Genes Are Nice But Joy Is Better', *Harvard Gazette*, April 2017. https://news. harvard.edu/gazette/ story/2017/04/over-nearly-80-years-harvard-study-has-been-showing-how-to-live-a-healthy-

and-happy-life/. Or for a very watchable report by the research head psychiatrist, Robert Waldinger (Harvard Study of Adult Development), https://vimeo.com/209196355.

2. Hassan, T., unpublished manuscript, 2018

3. For the UK picture, here is a good study: Booker, C. L., Kelly, Y. J. and Sacker, A. (2018), 'Gender differences in the associations between age trends of social media interaction and well-being among 10–15-year-olds in the UK', BMC Public HealthBMC series 201818:321, https://doi.org/10.1186/s12889-018-5220-4 © 20 March 2018.

4. https://www.theatlantic.com/magazine/archive/2017/09/has-the-smartphone-destroyed-a-generation/534198/

5. Twenge, J., *iGen: Why Today's Super-Connected Kids Are Growing Up Less Rebellious, More Tolerant, Less Happy – and Completely Unprepared for Adulthood (and What That Means for the Rest of Us)*, Simon and Schuster, 2018.

6. Suicide had been higher among teens several decades ago, but good mental health campaigns leading to greater awareness and support for kids and better use of anti-depressants in emergency situations had combined to reduce this progressively. But the rates, especially among young people, began to grow from 2010 despite this.

13: Girls and Their Mums

1. Parker, K. (13 January 2011), *A Portrait of Stepfamilies*, Pew Research Center report, http://pewsocialtrends.org/2011/01/13/a-portrait-of-stepfamilies/

2. Gibbs, N., 'The Magic of the Family Meal', *Time Magazine*, 4 June 2006. Kids who eat with their parent/s each night have stunningly better outcomes (though it's possible the family meal is an expression of a family being calm, ordered and friendly as much as a cause). Eating together produces oxytocin, the hormone that makes people like each other. The research also found its the *regularity* of having family meals that does the trick, (at least, for the evening meal of the day). Try it for a month, and see for yourself.

14: Girls and Their Dads

1. My turn. Biddulph, S., *The New Manhood*, Finch, 2010.

2. Greer, G., *The Whole Woman*, Anchor, 2000.

Contributors and Acknowledgements

Paula Joye is a journalist and fashion writer. She was formerly the editor of *Cleo* and *Madison* magazines, and is currently editor of www. lifestyled.com.au and the Fashion and Style columnist for Fairfax Media.

Kim McCabe is the founder and director of Rites for Girls and a mother of three. She studied child psychology at Cambridge University, was a counsellor to young people, and taught sex education in schools and youth groups. She was determined to find a way to equip girls so they would traverse their teen years happily and well. She lives in Forest Row, Sussex, England, and trains leaders worldwide in the Girls Journeying Together programme.

Dr Michael Carr-Gregg is Australia's best-known psychologist and authority on adolescent mental health. He founded the national organisation for teenage cancer patients, CanTeen, is Associate Professor at the University of Melbourne's Department of Paediatrics, and created the National Centre Against Bullying (www.ncab.org.au). Michael is the author of *Surviving Adolescents* (2005), *The Princess Bitchface Syndrome* (2006), *Real Wired Child* (2007) *Surviving Step Families* (2011), *Surviving Year 12* (2012) and *When to Really Worry* (2010).

Melinda Tankard Reist is an Australian feminist, media commentator and advocate for women and girls. Melinda is author of *Giving Sorrow Words* (2000), *Defiant Birth: Women Who Resist Medical Eugenics* (2006), *Getting Real: Challenging the Sexualisation of Girls* (2009), and co-editor with Abigail Bray of *Big Porn Inc: Exposing the Harms of the Global Pornography Industry* (2011), all published by Spinifex Press. (www.melindatankardreist.com)

Lydia Jade Turner is a psychotherapist specialising in eating disorders and unhealthy weight loss behaviours. In addition she works with those affected by bariatric surgery, 'obesity', sexual assault, trauma, and gender-related difficulties. A staunch critic of the diet industry, Lydia regularly presents at conferences worldwide She is the Manager of Advocacy, Education & Social Health at BodyMatters Clinic. (www.bodymatters.com.au)

Sarah McMahon is a psychologist who specialises in the treatment of eating disorders. She is the Manager of Clinical & Consultancy Services at BodyMatters Clinic in Sydney Australia. Sarah has over a decade's experience in counselling people affected by disordered eating behaviours, facilitating eating disorder support groups and educating the community about eating pathology, in corporations, public hospitals, non-government organisations and private practice. (www.bodymatters.com.au)

Paul Dillon is Australia's foremost drug and alcohol educator. His best-selling book *Teenagers, Alcohol and Drugs* was released in 2009. Paul wrote the instruction manual for the NSW Police Services on alcohol and violence, and developed the United Nations UNODC Global Youth Training Workshop on amphetamine use among young people. For information on Paul's work go to http://darta.net.au/

Maggie Hamilton is a New Zealand-based writer, social researcher and publisher who has campaigned widely about the deteriorating mental health of girls. Her books include *What's Happening to Our Girls?* (2009), and *What's Happening to Our Boys?* (2011). Her most recent book aimed at girls is *Secret Girls Business* (2012), a beautifully crafted guide to creativity and individuality as an antidote to conformity and competition. www.maggiehamilton.org

Collective Shout is a network of women professionals who campaign against the sexual exploitation of girls. Their friendship and inspiration made this book a far better one. You can subscribe or get involved at collectiveshout.org

Micky Foss is a psychotherapist and mother in Lismore, Australia. She specialises in Gestalt, Family and couples therapy.

Dr Bruce Robinson is the author of *Daughters and their Dads, and Fathering From the Fast Lane* (2001). He is a thoracic physician, a professor of medicine, and the author of over 150 published papers. Bruce founded The Fathering Project at the University of Western Australia, and speaks about fatherhood around the globe. The Project's very moving DVD 'What Kids Really Need From Their Dads' greatly influenced me as a dad, and is a great resource for encouraging fathers. www.thefatheringproject.org

I especially wish to thank Kathy Dyke, Carolyn Thorne and Simon Gerratt at HarperCollins UK, and all editors, typesetters and translators worldwide for their work on this new edition.

Julie Gale at Kids Free 2B Kids. Johanna. Linda Dalton, Arne Rubenstein. Caroline Richards. Kate Hadwen. Esther Kennedy, Lauris Pandolfini, Jane Bezzina and Ramesh Manocha for all those amazing seminars. Ariana Biddulph for research assistance, a scientific mind-set, and teaching me to laugh in adverse circumstances! And Kirsty McGeoch for first telling my about Peter Benson and the idea of Spark.

To Kim John Payne. To Doro Marden. To Shaaron, for showing me how.

And to Kaycee, Marielle, Genevieve, and their families. Well done.

About the Illustrator

Kimio Kubo is a young Japanese-born artist who lives with his family in a remote rainforest community near Bellingen NSW. His drawings of family scenes have brought acclaim for their sensitive, piercing and touching depictions of family life. Contact details: Kimio Kubo, PO Box 45 Thora, NSW 2454, Australia.

Steve Biddulph's website is at: www.stevebiddulph.com